OXFORD
SERMONS

VOLUME III

HUPOMONE PRESS
FORT WORTH, TEXAS

©2009 by Hupomone Press, Fort Worth, Texas
All rights reserved.
ISBN: 978-1-61623-836-0
Printed in the United States of America.

Library of Congress Cataloging-in-Publication Data
Oxford Sermons 2009/Dr. Joel C. Gregory, gen. ed., 1948-
Includes index.
ISBN: 978-1-61623-836-0

DEDICATION

TO DR. RALPH DOUGLAS WEST SR.
FOUNDER AND SENIOR PASTOR OF
THE CHURCH WITHOUT WALLS
HOUSTON, TEXAS

———— ⚬∿⚬ ————

One who exemplifies the disciplines of the

Proclaimers Place

PREFACE

For the third time, some participants of Proclaimers Place in Oxford have joined together to present a collection of sermons to ministers and laypersons. Those proclaiming these messages attended the 2009 Proclaimers Place seminar in Oxford. These messages articulate the distinctive voice and experience of the individual preachers involved in this unique series of meetings. These ministers shared in common a time of studying biblical exegesis, hermeneutics, and homiletics at Regent's Park College, Oxford University. Including the proclaimers participating this year, those who have enjoyed the Oxford experience now number 126.

Special gratitude belongs to Rev. Dr. William Crouch, president of Georgetown College, and Rev. Dr. Rob Ellis, principal of Regent's Park College. These two Christian gentlemen, each of whom belongs to the board of the other's institution, have opened the doors to Regent's Park and the opportunity to study in that academic environment.

The format of Proclaimers Place has remained the same in outline for the nine seminars held over five years at Oxford as well as for the 32 seminars held in the United States. The seminar participants examine one biblical text per day, first studying the exegesis of the text and then the crafting of a sermon after that. The Oxford experience in 2009 played a variation on that theme. The seminar attendees studied a text from the preaching of Joseph Parker on Tuesday morning and then traveled to his church, the City Temple of London, on Tuesday afternoon. On Friday the participants studied a text from the preaching of John R. W. Stott in the morning and traveled to his church in London (All Souls Langham Place) that afternoon. This contextualized the preaching of these two noteworthy London preachers.

The concept of Proclaimers Place involves the study of preaching by exploring individual texts and then allowing them to raise questions about the discipline of exegesis and the craft of homiletics. To a degree this might be called an inductive method of studying preaching in that we are looking at particulars rather than general concepts. The testimony of many participants has been that this style of studying the Word has helped their understanding of the task. Men and women from coast to coast and border to border and from many Christian traditions have enriched one another around the tables in the buildings overlooking the historic quad of Regent's Park College.

For me, the meetings at Oxford and the Proclaimers Place movement in general have been one of the most fulfilling of all ministerial endeavors. To sit with brothers and sisters in Christ and work together through the details of particular texts, share our insights, discuss every aspect of homiletics and enjoy the ambience of a great international center of learning creates memories that burn brighter every year. Many of us will cherish for a lifetime the friendships and conversations from these hallowed and treasured days together at Oxford in the summer.

So we present to you these messages. They have been edited only for the most basic essentials, with the distinctive voice and cadence of the individual proclaimers preserved throughout them. May the Word of God be heard clearly in each, and may that Word redeem and transform all of us.

—*Joel C. Gregory*

Distinguished Fellow

Georgetown College

Professor of Preaching

George W. Truett Theological Seminary

Baylor University

CONTENTS

Trusting God in Tough Times
(Job 13:15)

REV. HUGH BAIR, D. MIN., PH.D.

Christian Life Church
Baltimore, Maryland

Today, our world is changing and shifting. It is an age of newness—new things, new value systems, new moralities, and new people with new knowledge. It is an age of plastic people who are superficial and artificial: they are not for real, and they are not genuine or sincere. As a result, it is difficult to trust people. When Barack Obama gave his inauguration speech in Washington, D. C., in front of two million people on that cold day in January of 2009, he used the word "trust" in his very first sentence. When he brought up issues about trust, he was making a lot of sense, because trust has been in short supply in Washington in recent years. In the business world, we see the erosion of trust; institutions and executives once viewed as solid have been called into question. Pardon me for stating the obvious, but the whole issue of trust has not exactly been going well for us in this country. From investment adviser Bernard Madoff, who has been accused of stealing $50 billion, to an Illinois governor alleged of selling a Senate seat, we have serious issues regarding trust.

Within the context of our marriages, which should be built on trust, we are seeing issues involving betrayal of that trust. According to research surveys conducted from 1991 to 2006 by the National Science Foundation, however, the number of unfaithful wives under the age of 30 has increased by 20% and the number of unfaithful husbands by 45%.

Even in the environment of the church we are experiencing trust issues. In recent years, we have witnessed the stupidity of those in high places. We have seen too many moral financial shipwrecks among high-profile ministers. In short, we have serious issues about trust!

As a result:

- The world is in a jam.
- The nation is in a mess.
- The home is in trouble.
- The individual is in torment.

Stress is shattering the lives of so many people. Everybody is uptight, and tension is the order of the day. Loneliness and fear have not gone on vacation, either. No wonder we find ourselves in the midst of a post-modern trust crisis.

So, who can you trust? The front cover of the March 2009 issue of the *Oprah* magazine asks the question, "Who can you trust with your life, your money, your secrets, your man, and most of all—your hair!" Well, Oprah, there is somebody who I can place my trust in during tough times. Furthermore, as a result of placing my trust in this person, I am not help-less, clueless, or voiceless—and that person is God.

One thing I know is that Job demonstrated practical leadership in tough times; in fact, Job epitomized trust in difficult times. It is so easy to think that a story as old as Job's is familiar to everyone, but it may be new to you. So, allow me in a few lines to offer a quick synopsis of the life of Job.

Overnight, without warning, Job's world came tumbling down—to such a devastated state that he tore up the very clothes he was wearing. In one fell swoop, he was rendered childless by a traumatic and tragic situa-tion. Then, after being stricken by a terrible sickness, Job was tormented by his wife, who suggested that he needed to curse God and die. He was sneered at by his friends Zophar, Bildad, and Eliphaz. In fact, his three friends informed him that he must have done something wrong or God wouldn't be punishing him, so they called him a phony and a hypocrite. Life was difficult and unfair for him at times.

Just like Job, you too could go from fortune to misfortune, from calm to calamity, from blessing to cursing, from acceptance to rejection, and from prosperity to poverty. No one can argue the point that life is punctuated with hardships, heartaches, and headaches. Job sunk lower than any other person, yet he epitomized trust in difficult times by demonstrating consistency of character. Job's life is a great example of maintaining a solid trust in God, no matter what the circumstances are.

I have some questions for you:

- What was it about Job that enabled him to overcome his insurmountable problems?
- What was it that made Job so victorious when his world was falling apart?
- When Job experienced undeserved suffering, how was he able to make sense of his suffering?

I believe the answers to these questions can be found in the biblical text.

UNWAVERING TRUST IN GOD DURING THE MOST DIFFICULT SETBACKS OF LIFE

The first sentence of Job 13:15 has been interpreted in various ways. The scholarly variations of the text notwithstanding, this is undoubtedly one of the most famous lines in the Book of Job. Readers of the King James Version (KJV) of the Bible in every generation since 1611 have heard in their minds Job make this heroic declaration of faith: "Though he slay me, yet will I trust in him." The word "slay" means to assassinate, which sounds rather violent. Contextually and grammatically, of course, Job did not mean it literally because he was alive when he said it. He was using strong language because that's how he felt—as though God had struck him dead.

We only see Job sitting down on a heap of ashes, scraping off the corruption of the lingering sores all over his body. But Job saw nothing to cheer him—nothing to comfort or inspire him. Job saw nothing to light his way through the night of doubt and sorrow. But before he continued in his long night of pain, like a flash of lightning he received a revelation about his painful predicament. He declared and demonstrated that he was going to place his unwavering trust in God during the most difficult setback of his life. Job 1:21 states, "Naked came I out of my mother's womb, and naked shall I return thither: the Lord gave and the Lord hath taken away; blessed be the name of the LORD." In other words, nothing could alter Job's trusting affirmation, firm belief, and confidence in the honesty, integrity, reliability, and justice of God. He demonstrated this trusting relationship by worshipping. He did not wallow and wail; instead, he worshipped.

The Hebrew word for "blessed" means to recognize God, to kneel before God, to praise God, or to eulogize God. In the pit of suffering, Job spoke well of God in spite of his trials and difficulties. Do you know how Job overcame the attack of Satan and the difficulty of his situation? He trusted God without any reservation whatsoever, and he worshipped. He fell down upon the ground and worshipped!

- When you stumble and stagger from bad news to worse news, worship!
- When Satan wants to take you out with trouble and trials, worship!

- When others have buried you under a judgment of failure, worship!
- When you are overwhelmed by events and circumstances that are spinning out of control, worship!

Job said to us that no matter how harshly life had treated him, no matter how painful the disappointments were, no matter how rough the road he had travelled, no matter how poverty-stricken he became, even if God decided to slay him, he was going to demonstrate a trusting relationship with God by worshipping Him.

TURN YOUR SETBACKS INTO A COMEBACK BY TRUSTING IN GOD'S ABILITY

". . . Though he slay me, yet will I trust in him. . . ." I want us to look at the word "yet." It means "in spite of, in addition to, or on top of it all." "I will put my trust in God," said Job. After the word "yet" comes the affirmation and determination that nothing could prevent Job from being righteous before God. Nothing—no one, no circumstance, no event, no condition in life—nothing could interfere with Job's trust in God.

Look again at Job's miserable setbacks in life. He was stripped of wealth, stripped of children, stripped of health, stripped of his friends, and stripped of status and respect. So, the question that is before us is, How does Job turn his miserable setbacks into a comeback? We need to look at the text again: "Though he slay me, yet will I trust in him." The New International Version gives us a new perspective on what Job was saying: "Though he slay me, yet will I hope in him."

Job had what theologians call "existential hope." Existential hope is grounded in an experience in life upon which you can rely. In other words, out of your existential experience in the past you have called on God before, and He delivered you. Since God delivered you "back then," He can do it again.

Viktor Frankl, a psychiatrist and a Holocaust survivor, wrote about his experience in a Nazi concentration camp. He said, "Everything can be taken from a man but one thing: the last of human freedoms—to choose one's attitude in any given set of circumstances." * Holding on to hope in the midst of suffering will help a person find significance in living. Having a sense of hope in life is so necessary.

- Hope is as important as water is to a fish.
- Hope is as vital as electricity is to a light bulb.
- Hope is as essential as air is to a jumbo jet.

- Hope is basic to life!!
- We believe in a hope that will never fail.

We believe in the hope that . . .

- Science will be our helper and not our destroyer;
- A better day is coming in the morning; and
- Trouble won't last forever.

- To have hope means that you have the will to persist in spite of pessimism.
- To have hope means that you persist in spite of discouragement.
- To have hope means that you believe there is a solution—a way through every wilderness—and you have a hope that will not fail.

Let me see if I can define hope a little better:

The psychologist Erik Erikson, who advanced our understanding of human psychosocial development, characterized hope as a trust or confidence. In other words, an individual, through hope, can endure until his or her change comes.

- Hope does not accept the situation as it is; instead, it defies the negative.
- Hope says that I refuse to accept the reality of my situation.
- Hope does not abandon its post but hangs in there until a change comes.
- Hope extinguishes anxiety.
- Hope includes active involvement by the individual toward improvement in one's health.
- Hope believes that a turn for the better is on the way and God can change the circumstances.

Can I tell you what God's hope has done for me? I don't know about you, but all the bumps on the road of my life have turned out to be a blessing for me.

- All of my failures are still my teachers.
- All of my mistakes are still my major professors.
- All of my defeats have become my victories.

Holding on to hope involves the possibility of turning your miserable setbacks into comebacks.

FAITH IN GOD PRODUCES TRUST

Job was handed some bad news, so he had to face hard times. But Job said, ". . . but I will maintain mine own ways before him." He was basically saying, "I will keep doing what I have been doing." Every now and then, there will come a time when you have to ask yourself the following questions: Do I give up? Do I quit? Or, do I keep doing what I have been doing? In the end, we discover that Job's best days were still ahead of him. Why? Because he simply kept doing what he had been doing. What was Job doing during his time of sorrow and pain? He was maintaining his faith in God.

Your faith in God during difficult times has the capacity to take you to another level. The only reason why you haven't lost your mind is because your faith has given you the ability to trust God. Job was struggling because he was in a crisis. Sometimes a crisis can cause us to put our trust in something else rather than in God; however, we don't need a four-leaf clover or a rabbit's foot around our neck. What we need is faith in God during a crisis or a difficult situation. Faith in God makes us depend on God and not on others.

The reason that some of us are limited is because we have allowed other people to determine our outcome, which we should never do. We cannot allow people to define who we are by the labels they put on us. Faith in God helps us to understand that other people don't have the final word regarding our lives, but it is God who decides who we are.

What I like about Job is that he refused to be identified by the labels that were put upon him. His self-identity was not in his 7,000 sheep, 3,000 camels, 500 yoke of oxen, or 500 donkeys. Satan had made a mistake. He thought Job's identity was based on what he had or his money, but Job's identity was actually rooted in his relationship with God. So, even though Job lost everything he had, it did not stop him from trusting and worshipping God. Job never lost his faith. Instead, he maintained his integrity; as a result, God richly rewarded Job by doubling his material possessions, giving him more children, and allowing him to live a long life.

Would God do anything less for you if you are willing to trust Him? Job is our example of what God did for Job and will do for all who are willing to trust Him. Therefore,

- When you don't understand what's going on, trust God.
- When you cannot see the way, trust God.
- When you are in the midst of sorrow, trust God.

Whatever strength, wisdom, comfort, guidance, or help you may need, you can trust God. God may not explain why you are going through a certain situation, but rest assured that God will reveal Himself as the God whom you can trust. ⟳

* Victor Frankl, *Man's Search for Meaning* (Boston: Beacon Press, 2006), 9.

Can You Hear Me Now?
(Luke 1:20)

———⌒⌒———

BISHOP T. ANTHONY BRONNER

ELIM Christian Fellowship
Buffalo, New York

In this advanced age of cellular technology, one of the most familiar and popular phrases is "Can you hear me now?" This cell phone slogan suggests that the ability to hear, or comprehend, is essential to communication. For cell phone companies, the ability to hear is directly related to the range of coverage provided by the cellular network; but for God, the ability to hear is predicated only upon a willingness to listen. Marriages, friendships, and relationships of every sort suffer because of our unwillingness to listen. We just will not stop talking long enough to hear what others have to say. We think that what we have to say is far more important, so we overtalk or loud-talk everyone else.

Just as hearing is essential to communication and communication is essential to relationships, healthy relationships require bidirectional dialogue. We must engage in both receptive and expressive communication. In other words, we must be as committed to hearing as we are to being heard.

There is no relationship in which communication is more important than in the relationship between God and His people. Our willingness to hear is the most significant aspect of communicating with God, for faith comes by hearing.

Even though God is in the habit of speaking, we are not in the habit of listening. We talk to God, but we rarely allow (or even expect) God to talk to us. Often we claim that God has said this thing or that, when we have not actually bothered to listen to what God has really said. We have discovered that the secret to gaining people's trust is simply by prefacing our statements with, "And the Lord said," but this will not suffice with God. To fully participate in the plan of God, we must engage in active listening. If Adam had not been listening in Genesis 3:15 when God said that He would bring redemption by crushing the head of the Enemy with the foot of man, we would have missed the redevelopment of humanity. If Noah had not been listening when God told him to build an ark and wait for rain, there would have been no recovery for the Creation. If Moses had not been listening up on the mountain when God said to him, "Stand still and see My salvation," the children of Israel would still be on the wrong side of the Promised Land. So, while this lesson is intended to empower and impact leaders, perhaps it can also help laity and leadership alike to be in a position to hear the voice of God. If we do not learn to listen, we will miss God.

In the first chapter of Luke, there is a fellow by the name of Zacharias (also pronounced Zachariah) whose name means "remembering God" or "God remembers you." The two meanings are interchangeable as long as it is understood that the name involves both God and remembrance. Zacharias' posterity is anchored by two significant things: First, he is a priest. Second, he is the husband of Elizabeth, who is first cousin to Mary, the future mother of Jesus. It is this divine connection that establishes Zacharias' relationship with the holy family.

On this certain day Zacharias was the priest on duty, and it was his turn to go into the Holy Place to burn incense before the Lord—to communicate with God. Whereas we can now walk into the house of God with absolute freedom (so much that we often arrive late, haphazardly, and with irreverent familiarity), it is important to note that the priests of antiquity did not have this liberty. They did not have license to be in the presence of God at will. Rather, it was their custom to draw lots for the privilege of entering the Holy of Holies. Most priests spent their entire lifetime awaiting this chance, and many died before it was afforded them. So Zacharias did not stagger when given this once-in-a-lifetime opportunity. He had drawn the sacred lot, and this was his one shot to have an audience with God (Luke 1:8-9).

PRAYER ANSWERED

Zacharias understood that he could not speak to the people on God's behalf unless he had first spoken to God. During that time, revelatory knowledge could not be scooped out of books. It was neither born of ritualism nor acquired from the kind of discipline and routine study that makes men appear learned. Revelation only came from God. So on this exciting day in the life of Zacharias, God (by way of the angel Gabriel) spoke to him. This is, in essence, what God said: "Zacharias, I am going to answer your prayer! You have been talking to me, Zacharias. Now let Me talk to you. For years you have been telling Me that you and Elizabeth would like to have a child. You come into the temple time and time again to perform your priestly duties, and you never fail to mention that you would like to have a child. You have sought Me greatly. You have called upon Me. You have pursued Me, and now I am ready to respond to you. I am going to give you a son, and you will call him John."

PERPETUAL BLESSING

God's plan was to answer Zacharias' prayer so that he could be a source of perpetual blessing to the people of God. God and Zacharias were alone in the temple; no one else was there. There were no distractions or hindrances—just God assuring Zacharias of His promise. But

Zacharias was not listening, and he did not comprehend when God said, "Zacharias—your son will be unusual. He will not drink wine or strong drink. He will have the remarkable task of reuniting fathers with their children. He will change the economy and the social structure. He will bring absolute change to the environment. He will preach the gospel of repentance and will be the forerunner for the Savior. This is what you have been praying for, Zacharias. I am answering your prayers."

POOR PERCEPTION

It seems that Zacharias went into the Holy Place not actually expecting to find God there, because the presence of God frightened him. He was accustomed to talking to God, but he was not at all accustomed to hearing God or listening to Him. He heard about the child all right, but he missed the part about the child's role in the plan of salvation. His thinking was strictly anthropocentric. That is to say, he perceived things man's way rather than God's way. He could only consider that which was humanly possible. He could not see any way that he and Elizabeth could have a child in their old age. Perhaps if he had spent as much time listening to God as he had talking to God, he would have developed a theocentric way of thinking and would have understood that all things are possible with God. Instead, Zacharias replies, "Are You kidding me? A baby? Really? At my age? You should have done this many years ago. This should have happened a long time ago. It is not possible for You to do this thing now."

POWER AND PERSUASION

Can you imagine the shock on God's part? Here was Zacharias, a faith leader who lacked faith. Zacharias had been praying and seeking hard for this thing; and now that God was willing to grant his desire, he was not moved because *God's* timing was off. There was no celebration from Zacharias: no rejoicing, no sense of elation, nor any sign whatsoever of excitement over the answering of his prayer. His constant talking rendered him unable to hear God, which caused him to be faithless, for faith comes by hearing. He actually questioned or challenged God's ability to perform.

Though some would argue to the contrary, it does not bother God to be challenged *per se*. Abraham challenged God in Genesis 15 when he referred to the covenant. Gideon challenged God in Judges 6 when he asked God to do that fleece test. Also, Mary challenged God in the latter part of Luke 1 when she inquired about how she would have a child. We find that neither the challenge of Abraham, Gideon, nor Mary bothered God. They challenged God because they could not understand His methodology. Zacharias, on the other hand, challenged God because he did not believe in His ability to do what he perceived to be the impossible.

People mirror the mindset of their leaders, so Zacharias' faithlessness posed a risk to the entire community. Abraham was just starting out, Gideon was just putting out a fleece, and Mary was just a teenager. But Zacharias was an old, seasoned, veteran priest. His sphere of influence was far too great for him to hold any unbelief. Zacharias had power and authority; when he spoke, the people listened. According to the text, the people were standing outside the temple waiting for Zacharias to bring them a word from the Lord. Although Zacharias had not positioned himself to hear God, the people had positioned themselves to hear Zacharias. What if he came out with the wrong message? Just like today, leaders had the power to either speak life or speak death.

PUNISHMENT IMPOSED

Contrary to modern thinking, God does still punish, and Zacharias' faithlessness required punishment. Contemporary scholars prefer the word "chasten" over the word "punish," but both terms are essentially the same. God chastens or punishes out of love; in other words, His punishment is imposed so that there might be reconciliation or realignment of attitudes. Zacharias was completely out of alignment with God. He did not believe what he heard. He did not believe that God would perform that which He had said. Moreover, he did not believe that God would move right then—in that season. In short, Zacharias was not listening to God.

It is wrong for leaders to harbor unbelief while going through the routine and ritual of worship: organizing, delegating, and administrating without faith. Zacharias was swinging incense in the presence of God, but his lack of faith had the potential to cause an antithetical experience in the house of God. So Zacharias' mouth was shut by God because he did not believe in the Word. He was silenced because he did not believe in miracles. He was made speechless because he did not believe in God's timing.

At any rate, Zacharias had fallen short. His punishment was severe, but it was only for nine months. Considering the number of years he had spent praying without expectation of any answer, nine months was a relatively short period of time. Zacharias spent many, many years talking to God, but he never stopped talking long enough to hear God. So, in Luke 1:20, God tells him that for as long as it takes for this to happen ". . .you shall be dumb. . ." (In other words, stop talking—just listen.)

PROVIDENCE OF GOD

Even though Zacharias fell short and experienced a severe punishment for a short period of time, he was still God's chosen man. When God sets something in motion, it cannot be changed, not even by Him. Once God speaks, it has to happen. John had to be the child of Zacharias and Elizabeth, just like Jesus had to be born through Mary. This had been providentially laid out, so it had to come to pass. Likewise, our anthropocentric mess-ups may disrupt the schedule, but we cannot derail the plan of God. In Numbers 13, for example, there were 10 leaders who spoke against the Promised Land blessing. Although they slowed things down a bit, they most certainly did not stop anything. There is a disciple by the name of Judas who talked against Jesus whom the Romans crucified. That slowed things down, but on Sunday morning He arose with all power, so the course of events went according to plan. Here is the point: God determined that Zacharias would go down in history as an esteemed figure. Despite his disbelief, when the time was right, when the season came, and when the appointed time arrived, *God remembered Zacharias.*

PERFECTED PRAISE

Zacharias withstood his punishment. During this time of silence his perception improved to the point that he was able to hear and align himself with God. As he came into alignment with God's perspective, he was also able to accept God's desire to answer his prayers and his place in perpetuity. Of equal importance was the fact that Zacharias was now able to communicate the will of God to his wife: When the time came for the naming of their baby, Elizabeth understood him when he insisted that the child was to be called John. By naming the child John, Zacharias (and Elizabeth) demonstrated complete acceptance of the will and authority of God. Then, in accordance with the providence of God, Zacharias' voice was restored; and he powerfully and persuasively praised God. Essentially, he said, "The Lord is my light and my salvation, whom shall I fear?(Ps. 27:1). The Lord is my shepherd, I shall not want (Ps. 23:1). I shall go through the fire and not be burned. I shall go through the waters and not drown (Isa. 43:2). God will bring the high places down and the valleys up high (Isa. 40:4). The Lord will do exceedingly and abundantly above that which I could ask or think (Eph. 3:20). Let everything that hath breath praise the Lord! (Ps. 150:6). "

God is still asking, "Can you hear Me now?" Can you hear God? Do you recognize His voice, or must your spirit be quieted first? It was the Jewish custom to name the first male child after his father, but God had instructed Zacharias to name his child John. Somehow, despite his dumbness (his speechlessness) Zacharias managed to relay that directive to Elizabeth, and she complied. The significance of this exchange of information between Zacharias and his wife regarding the naming of their child is that when leaders are in alignment with God, they can successfully communicate His will to those over whom they have authority.

God is still calling us to be leaders today, but we must be able to hear and distinguish the voice of God in order to convey the will of God to the people of God. As leaders, we are not expected to be perfect. We have all had some dumb moments (pun intended), said some dumb things, done some dumb deeds, visited some dumb places, and been with some dumb people; but we are expected to recognize and regard the voice of God. If we remember God, however, He will remember us. That which God has set in motion on our behalf will then come to pass, and we will see His promises in this season.

A Yet Praise
(Habakkuk 3:17-19)

DR. JERRY M. CARTER JR.

Calvary Baptist Church
Morristown, New Jersey

One of the most amazing miracles of human history was the way slaves of the antebellum South were able to come together and worship God excitedly and energetically in the midst of damnable and despicable conditions. They had very few external signs that God was on their side. It would have been easy for them to be swallowed up in bitterness and the dark night of the soul.

These slaves had been dehumanized on every front. They were snatched from their homeland, forced to work from sunup to sundown, and paid nothing. Their families were often torn apart: some worked on one plantation, while other members of the family were sent to another. It would have been easy to give up on God.

But somehow or another, they were able to produce songs and praise that contradicted what they were going through. They would go to church on Sunday with their masters and tolerate the services. But that night, they gathered down by the riverside and really got "their praise on" in what E. Franklin Frazier calls the Invisible Institution. The spirit of what these slaves were able to do is very much connected to the spirit of the prophet in this particular text.

Habakkuk 3:17-19 has been called one of the greatest expressions of faith in all of the Bible, even though the Scriptures are filled with classic statements and affirmations of faith:

- "Though he slay me, yet will I trust in him" (Job 13:15);
- "But they that wait upon the Lord shall renew their strength. They shall mount up with wings as eagles; run and not be weary; walk and not faint" (Isa. 40:31);
- "Trust in the Lord with all thine heart, lean not to thine own

understanding. In all thy ways acknowledge him, and he shall direct thy path" (Prov. 3:5); and

- "....For I know in whom I have believed, and am persuaded that he is able to keep that which I have committed unto him against that day" (2 Tim. 1:12).

All of these verses are strong statements, but this one in Habakkuk stands head and shoulders above them all.

COMPLAINTS IN THE BEGINNING VS. CELEBRATION AT THE END

This verse is called an inimitable statement of faith because it reaffirms the fact that the real genius of faith lies in its ability to stand up in the midst of struggle. One's level of faith is not determined by what faith does in prosperity; instead, it is determined by what faith does in adversity. You really don't know how much faith you have until you experience adversity.

Habakkuk 3:17-19 is a strong expression of faith. However, faith is not necessarily expressed throughout this whole book. There is some doubt expressed in this book. There are some complaints in this book. There are questions regarding theodicy in this book; that is to say, there is some questioning about God's justice.

There are some arguments with God in this book. At first, it appears as though God was not on the side of His people: They had been taken captive by the Babylonians, and many of them were exiled to Babylon. The land of Judah had been destroyed by the invaders. Their crops were failing and their livestock dying. Holy places had been desecrated. Those who were not on God's side were prospering. Consequently, the prophet wondered whether or not the LORD had gone on vacation, leaving them to fend for themselves.

Habakkuk commenced his speech with the question, "How long shall I cry and you not hear?" When you're going through certain trials, it helps to know *how long*. It's not *what* you're going through but *how long* you must go through it. *How long* will the pain last? *How long* will the turmoil be? You can handle certain experiences if you just know *how long* you have to endure them.

Habakkuk is distressed throughout the book, but at the end of the day he is able to say in verses 17 and 18 of this chapter, "Although the fig tree shall not blossom, neither shall fruit be in the vines; the labour of the olive shall fail, and the fields shall yield no meat; the flock shall be cut off from the fold, and there shall be no herd in the stalls: Yet I will rejoice in the LORD, I will joy in the God of my salvation."

Notice that all of Habakkuk's complaints and questions were in the beginning of the book. Likewise, it's not necessarily how you feel about the Lord at the beginning of the day that is most important: it's how you feel at the end of the day. It's all right to get down on your knees with despair and doubt; but when you get up off of your knees, you ought to be able to say with the prophet, "Although. . ., yet. . ."

Habakkuk is somehow able to release toward heaven a *yet* praise by the time we get to the end of the book. The prophet finishes on a new level of joy. He goes from complaint to celebration, with prayer in between; that's the bridge between the two. Indeed, the only way to move from complaint to celebration is through communion with the Almighty.

In that time of communication, you can be honest with God. You can cry, complain, and even curse if you want to because God can handle all that. In the process, however, God can transform all of that negativity into praise.

Before anything else, Habakkuk, channeling '60s singer Marvin Gaye, tells us "what's going on." Verse 17 reveals what the circumstances are. Habakkuk says, "The fig tree is not yielding any figs, there are no grapes, there are no olives, there is no grain, there are no sheep, and the cattle are dying." The people couldn't make it without these things. These were not niceties; these were necessities.

The prophet was aware of the situation—he was not blind to it. This was not some other-worldly mindset that allowed him to come up with a *yet* praise. He had a view about what was going on, but he was able to say, ". . .yet will I rejoice in the LORD."

Many times we think that we can only give God praise if we forget about what we are going through, but this only becomes escapism and not worship. Real worship acknowledges that the fig tree is not blossoming and the vine is not producing any grapes. The olive crop fails. The fields produce no food. There are no sheep in the pen and no cattle in the stalls.

You don't have to forget about trouble; you just recognize that there is something else going on in addition to what you are going through. In other words, you don't have to live in denial in order to be able to glorify God.

"ALTHOUGH. . .YET" VS. "SINCE. . .THEN"

Habakkuk tells us "what's going on." The people were going through a season of *unfulfilled expectations*. They expected the crops to come through and produce. They expected the sheep and cattle to flourish. *They were in a season when there were no visible signs that God was on their side.* The production of crops and the growth of flocks were signs of divine favor. (Unfortunately, just like we do, they measured the level of

God's favor by what they had, which is always a dangerous thing!) Habakkuk saw no signs of divine favor. Chaos was everywhere.

Have you ever been there? Have you ever had a season of unfulfilled expectations? As much as we talk about divine favor, there are seasons when no visible signs of divine favor appear. We call them seasons of barrenness.

Like the prophet of old, we too have a list of although's:

- Although businesses are downsizing;
- Although the cost of living is increasing and employment is decreasing;
- Although we elected the candidate for change, and we're fighting the president against it;
- Although global warming is wreaking havoc in the world;
- Although our young men and women are dying in Afghanistan;
- Although racism is rearing its ugly head;
- Although I've had to deal with heartbreak in my own life as I've watched loved ones pass away; and
- Although bills are high and money is low. . .

Yet will I praise God!

Habakkuk explains what is going on. Then, he tells us what his reaction is, and this is what is crucial. *It does not simply involve what is going on, but it is how I am reacting to what is going on that will make the difference.* He says, "Although there are no figs, no grapes, and no olives; no sheaves of grain; no sheep; and the cattle are dying . . .yet will I rejoice in the LORD." His reaction is, "Although. . .yet."

It's not, "Since. . .then. . ." His reaction is not, "Since the fig tree is not blossoming, then I will walk around with my head down." It is, "although. . .yet."

"Although" and *"yet"* mean that my external scenario will not dictate my internal condition. It means that my spirit is rebelling against my situation. "Although" admits things are bad. "Yet" acknowledges, "I ain't goin' to jump off the bridge."

The prophet goes on to say in verse 18, "Yet I will rejoice in the LORD, I will joy in the God of my salvation." The meaning of the words "rejoice" and "will joy" are interesting. *Alaz*, the Hebrew word for "rejoice" in this text, literally means to jump for joy. "Will joy" in this text literally means "to spin around under the influence of violent emotion." Habakkuk says, "Although the fig tree is not blossoming and the vine is producing no grapes, the olive crop fails, the fields produce no food, there are no sheep in the pen and no cattle in the stalls; *yet*, I will jump and spin."

Wait a minute! Crops are failing. Flocks and herds are dwindling. People are dying. Yet, the prophet is going to jump and spin?

I realize this does not sound sophisticated to us—jumping and spinning. It sounds more like the latest aerobic class. What are those prophets doing, jumping and spinning? I thought that when you got a position in the church, all of the jumping and spinning was over. I thought that once you became a preacher, deacon, deaconess, or trustee, all the jumping and spinning stopped. I thought that only those emotionally unstable folks were supposed to jump and spin. I thought that only ignorant, uneducated people did that jumping and spinning stuff. But Habakkuk would say to us, "Y'all can say what you want to about me. Right now I am going to jump and spin!"

"YET" PRAISE VS. "BECAUSE OF" PRAISE

The most amazing thing about this is that Habakkuk felt this way in light of what he was going through. This is what I call a *yet* praise. A *yet* praise is a praise that is not supposed to happen. A *yet* praise is a praise that does not make sense to people around you. They know what you are going through, *yet* they see you waving your hands and praising God. A *yet* praise is a praise that has you coming to church when you feel like you have every reason not to come. A *yet* praise has you singing when you just lost your job. A *yet* praise has you clapping after you just came from the doctor with a bad report. A *yet* praise will have you lifting up holy hands even when people are tearing you down. A *yet* praise will have you shouting "Hallelujah" even when you are broke.

Many of us are pretty good at *because* of praise, and we ought to praise God *because of*. He's worthy to be praised *because* He put food on the table, *because* He blessed me with a promotion, *because* He is enlarging my territory, *because* He healed my body, *because* He blessed me with a new car or house, *because* my income is increasing, or *because* He has given me victory over my enemies.

The psalmist says, "Praise ye the Lord. Praise God in his sanctuary; praise him in the firmament of his power. Praise him for his mighty acts: praise him according to his excellent greatness." Anytime you read, "Praise him 'for,' " that is *because* of praise, and that is all right too.

There is *because* of praise all through the Bible:

- Miriam and her girls got their tambourines, ran out to the street, and started blessing God because the LORD opened up the Red Sea.
- David danced out of his clothes on the street because he was able to bring the ark back to his city.
- Nehemiah and the people praised God so loudly that they could

be heard all over Jerusalem because they had finished rebuilding the walls.

- In Acts 3 there was a man in the temple who turned the church inside out by leaping and praising God because he had been healed after Peter touched him.

- A woman fell at Jesus' feet, and washed His feet with her tears and dried them with her hair because He had given her a brand-new life. All of this is *because* of praise.

However, there are times when no matter how hard you look, no matter how hard you try, you can't muster up any *because* of praise. You look around and you can't find any visible reason to worship the name of the LORD.

You look at yourself—no reason. You look at your money—no reason. You look at your health—no reason. You look at your job—no reason. You look at your family—no reason. You even look at your church—no reason. You search high and low, but you can't find a *because of* praise.

At that point, you need to bless God with a *yet* praise. *Christian maturity moves you from* because of *to* yet.

The Bible shows us something about a *yet* praise:

- A friend of mine lost his flocks, finances, family, his flesh, and the fidelity of his wife, but he said, "The Lord giveth and the Lord taketh away, blessed be the name of the Lord" (Job 1:21). That is a *yet* praise.

- The psalmist said, "I will bless the Lord at all times; his praise shall continually be in my mouth" (Psalm 34:1). That is a *yet* praise.

- Paul and Silas were in a Philippian jail, but at midnight they prayed and sang praises (Acts 16:25). That is a *yet* praise.
- The apostle John was exiled to the painfully lonely island of Patmos. There, he said, "I was in the Spirit on the Lord's day" (Rev. 1:9). That is a *yet* praise.
- "Count it all joy when you fall into various trials," says James 1:2. That is a *yet* praise.

A *yet* praise gives God the glory even when all hell is breaking loose in your life. A *yet* praise magnifies God even when you see no evidence of divine favor.

Habakkuk, you have to explain to me the reasons for your reaction. How were you able to muster up a *yet* praise? How can you muster up a *yet* praise when life is crazy? Habakkuk, according to the text, was able to come up with this kind of praise because *his focus was on the person of the Lord.* He says, "I will rejoice in the LORD, I will joy in the God of my salvation." "In the LORD" means that the LORD is the object of my praise and He is the location for my praise.

Habakkuk says, "I know that the fig tree is not blossoming. I know that the vines are producing no grapes. I know the olive crop fails. I know the fields aren't yielding any food. I know there are no sheep in the pen. I know there are no cattle in the stalls. But I am not focusing on that. My focus is on the LORD. And He's worthy of praise, whether there are figs or not; whether there are grapes or not." *You might not be able to find a reason to praise and worship in anything else, but you can always look toward the One who is from everlasting to everlasting.*

If the prophet was rejoicing in figs and olives, then his reason for rejoicing was now over. But Habakkuk was not focusing on the figs; he was focusing on the Giver of the figs. "In the LORD" means that Habakkuk's trouble is not the only thing that he is *in*: he is also "in the LORD." When you are *in Christ*, you are always in more than the situation you are *in*; so you are not just *in trouble*, but you are also in *the LORD*. Thus, you can offer a *yet* praise.

Habakkuk was able to give a *yet* praise because he was *leaning on the power of the* LORD. He says, "The LORD God is my strength." He does not say, "The LORD gives me strength." The LORD actually became in Habakukk what he could not be himself. So, even when he did not feel like praising God, the LORD actually became his strength to worship. When Habakkuk did not feel like going on, the Lord became his "going on."

When you don't feel like raising your hands in praise, God will do that for you. When you feel like quitting, God will actually be your strength. What God wants you to have, God becomes. God doesn't risk giving you strength; He becomes strength. That is how you are able to make it when you feel like you can go no farther.

Finally, Habakkuk was able to come up with a *yet* praise because he was *trusting in the provision of the* LORD. What was God providing? A *future*! The psalmist said, ". . .he will make my feet like hind's feet." The hooves of the hind, a female deer, enable her to climb the rocky, craggy mountainside in order to escape any danger. The doe not only could stand on high places but also could walk and live in high places. The only way that the deer could make it to the top was by planting her feet on the rough, rugged places on the mountainside. A smooth mountainside would not have enabled the deer to make it to the high places.

Habakkuk says, "I'm climbing the rough side of the mountain, but it is only so that I can make it to the top." Every now and then, the Lord will allow the way to get a little rugged, but it is just for the sake of elevation. I don't throw in the towel when the terrain gets rough because I know that my tribulation is the prelude to elevation. What the prophet is going through is necessary to get him where God wants him to be.

This is why Habakkuk was able to come up with a *yet* praise. Today we have two kinds of praisers in the house: the *because of* praisers and the *yet* praisers. Indeed, we ought to praise the Lord *because* He is a way-maker. He blesses us every day. But every now and then you have to muster up a *yet* praise. Although the fig tree shall not blossom. . .*yet* will I praise the LORD! ⚬⁄⚬

A Message in Miracles
(John 9)

PASTOR GEORGE W. DUBOIS

Evangelistic Temple Community Church
Buffalo, New York

The miracles recorded in John's Gospel account of Jesus' earthly ministry are pregnant with truths about the divine nature of Jesus. There is a message with every miracle that points to His divinity. For example, in the second chapter, Jesus turned water into wine at a wedding in Cana. This miracle conveys the message that Jesus can take things that are ordinary and turn them into things that are delightful, extraordinary, and elegant. Similarly, Jesus' divinity is revealed in the miracle chronicled in chapter 4. This chapter introduces us to a thirsty woman whose life had been turned upside down. Her relationships with six different men had failed, so she was in desperate need of hope. Jesus' dialogue with this woman at the well inspired her with a new energy and zeal to live again. He turned her desert into an oasis, revealing His divine character as the WATER OF L-I-F-E! Another aspect of Jesus' divine nature is recorded in chapter 11. This chapter explains how Jesus' friend Lazarus died. Jesus showed up and called him back from death and the grave. Following this miracle, He declared that He was the resurrection and the life. Again, there is a message about Christ's divinity (don't miss it) in every miracle documented in the apostle John's Gospel.

What we also need to know is that often times in the biblical narratives, individual afflictions or physical ailments are signs of the spiritual condition of a nation or community. For instance, in the Old Testament, the prophet Hosea's marriage to a prostitute symbolized Israel's whoring after other gods. Furthermore, barren women were often indicative of Israel's lack of productiveness and spiritual decay.

John 9, the focus of this sermon, supports this concept: physical ailments are signs of spiritual decay, and the miracles Jesus performed are filled with truths about His divine nature. In the text before us is a physically blind man. He is a product of a spiritually blind community that is in need of Jesus, the Light of the world. As I examined what the apostle John wrote about this community, I realized that the African proverb, "it takes a village to raise a child," applies to their situation: If the village is blind (spiritually), the children will be blind. If the village is lost, the children will be lost.

WE ALL HAVE BLIND SPOTS

Jesus said that when the blind leads the blind, all will fall in the ditch. It appears that everyone in the community where the blind man was born and raised in suffered from some type of blindness: 1) a man born blind (v.1); 2) neighbors in the community who were blind (v. 8); 3) parents who were blind (vv. 20-22); and 4) Pharisees who were blind (vv. 15-16).

The truth is that all of us have blind spots. I became acutely aware of blind spots while driving one day on the 33 Expressway in Buffalo, New York. I wanted to switch lanes and proceeded to do so by looking into both my rearview and side mirrors. As I changed lanes, however, I heard a motorist frantically honking her horn. She had to swerve to keep from hitting my car. I did not see her car because the vehicle was traveling in what is called a "blind spot."

In life, all of us from time to time suffer from blind spots. There are some things we just can't see. Just as I did not see the vehicle behind my car, the community that the blind man lived in did not recognize the cause of his disability. Let's explore what characterizes spiritually blind communities.

CHARACTERISTICS OF SPIRITUALLY BLIND COMMUNITIES

1. *Blind communities will focus on symptoms and not causes.* Verse 8 informs us that the community in which the blind man lived viewed him as a beggar. However, begging was only a symptom and not the real cause of this man's blindness. It is unfortunate that in many of our communities, we only see and treat symptoms but not the causes of our problems.

2. *Blind communities are filled with fault-finders.* For instance, in verse 2, the apostles asked Jesus, "Master, who did sin, this man, or his parents, that he was born blind?" The disciples wanted to blame someone. Whether it was this man or his parents, someone was at fault. Likewise, this community complained or found fault with Jesus healing the blind man on the Sabbath. Upon witnessing this miracle, the community said, "That's not our custom." We should be careful to look at what God is doing rather than just finding faults. We should not become so focused on the doom and gloom of life that we miss the power of God! God is always doing something in our community.

WHAT HAPPENS WHEN JESUS SHOWS UP IN A BLIND COMMUNITY?

It is evident that the first thing Jesus does is focus on the causes and not the symptoms. Unlike the community, Jesus saw a MAN born blind. This act not only shows that Jesus focuses on causes, but it also demonstrates that He will never confuse an adjective with a noun: Jesus saw a man (noun) who was blind (adjective). Contrary to this, the community saw a blind (adjective) and needy (adjective) man. When Jesus restored the blind man's sight, He showed that symptoms are temporary situations and not permanent conditions. To put it differently, the man was not blind because he was a beggar; he was a beggar because he was blind. Once Jesus cured his blindness, the man was no longer a beggar. Because of God's grace and mercy, Jesus looks beyond our adjectives (faults) and sees our needs and problems as opportunities for God to reveal both His power and glory.

As we further examine John 9, we learn a few things about God in this particular process of restoring sight. First, the text suggests that God can see us when we can't see Him. In verse 1, Jesus saw the blind man when the blind man could not see Him. Often in the storms of life, we cannot see God moving and working, but thank God that He can see us in our struggles and pain when we cannot see Him.

Second, the text lets us know that God has a miracle for your situation. His miracles meet our needs, whatever they might be. Jesus anointed the eyes of the blind man with a substance composed of His saliva and dirt. After the blind man followed Jesus' command to go wash in the pool of Siloam, his sight was restored. Jesus had provided a miracle to meet his needs. The synoptic Gospels are rich with other examples: At the wedding in Cana, Jesus turned water into wine. The woman with the issue of blood was healed once she touched the hem of His garment. When the apostle Peter needed money for his taxes, Jesus provided a fish with the coin in its mouth. For the woman caught in adultery, He silenced her critics. Our elders taught us that Jesus is water in dry places, bread in a starving land, and a bridge over troubled waters. Whatever we need, if we trust in Him, He will provide!

Finally, chapter 9 shows that the blind man obeyed Jesus. I often wonder how he made it to the pool in spite of his blindness. The blind man, however, just obeyed Jesus without seeing the road ahead. This is how faith operates: as we walk by faith in God's Word, He heals us and gives us a progressive revelation of His Son, as well as a testimony of His power.

The blind man's view of Jesus changes from verses 11 to 38: the blind man first calls Jesus a man in verse 11, then a prophet in verse 17, and finally Lord in verse 38. He is transformed from a beggar to a witness of the power of God after he recognizes Jesus as Lord. When asked about his opinion of Jesus, he stated, "Before I met Him, I was blind. Now that I've been with Him, I can see." I am sure he could agree with the lyrics of the Christian hymn, "Amazing Grace": "Amazing grace! How sweet the sound/That saved a wretch like me!/ I once was lost but now am found,/ Was blind but now I see." ❧

Storm Survivors
(Mark 4:35-41)

PASTOR FREDRICK L. FAIRLEY SR.

Berean Church
Phoenix, Arizona

Hurricane Katrina came ashore on the morning of Monday, August 29, 2005 in southeast Louisiana. It was one of the five deadliest, as well as one of the costliest, hurricanes in the history of the United States. It caused severe destruction along the Gulf Coast from central Florida to Texas. The most severe damage occurred in New Orleans, Louisiana, which flooded as the levee system catastrophically failed. As a result, there were more than one million internally displaced persons from the Gulf States region.

In the wake of Hurricane Katrina, a debate began after the news media referred to those who had to abandon their homes and cities as "refugees." On Friday, September 2, 2005, the Congressional Black Caucus held a news conference at the National Press Club. Representative Carolyn Kilpatrick, a Democrat from Detroit, declared, "These people are not refugees; they are American citizens." Vigorous debates began among editors and journalists. The National Association of Black Journalists encouraged editors to "choose more accurate terms, such as 'evacuees,' 'victims,' or even 'survivors.' "

As I listened to the debates and discussions, I too agreed that they were not refugees. Refugees are persons fleeing from political persecution, and they were certainly not doing that. They were also called "evacuees," but that still does not speak to the scope of their plight and problem. They were, without question, "storm survivors." They not only had come *to* a storm, but they also had come *through the* storm. I know some people and pastors, along with some saints and servants, whom I also would call "storm survivors"—not because they have survived the storms of nature, but because they have survived the storms of life.

If you have ever had to survive when your month was longer than your money, you are a storm survivor. If you have ever had to survive hell in your own family or ruptures in your relationships, you are a storm survivor. If you have ever had to provide leadership in a fellowship that had no follow-ship, you are a storm survivor. Your storm may not be tracked by CNN. Your storm may not make the pages of USA Today. Your storm may not be known by anyone except you and God; nonetheless, you are a storm survivor.

As you read Mark 4:35-41, you will discover that storms are not predictable. The writer said, "There arose a great storm." This phrase suggests that the storm came unexpectedly. The Sea of Galilee lies 680 feet below sea level. It is surrounded by hills, especially on the east side where they reach 2,000 feet high. These heights are a source of cool, dry air. Often the cool air descending from the hills will collide with the hot air that is ascending, causing a storm to manifest in an instant.

Life is often like that: before you know it, you are in a storm. One phone call—and you are in a storm. One e-mail—and you are in a storm. One trip to the doctor— and suddenly you are in a storm. Storms are not predictable.

Although they are not predictable, storms are certainly purposeful because it is in the storms of life that God measures our faith. In verse 40, after Jesus had calmed the storm, He asked His disciples, "Why are you so fearful? How is it that you have no faith?" Storms will reveal whether we are living in fear or living by faith. Fear is a state of anxiety and alarm due to an expectation of harm, but faith involves a complete reliance on God to do what is best for us in every situation. That is why faith and fear cannot exist in the same space. We must either come to the storm in fear or come through the storm in faith.

In his book *The Meaning of Faith*, the late Dr. Harry Emerson Fosdick says, "Fear imprisons, faith liberates; fear paralyzes, faith empowers; fear disheartens, faith encourages; fear sickens, faith heals; fear makes useless, faith makes serviceable." * The only way to survive your storm is by placing your faith and complete reliance in Jesus. Jesus is the only one who can handle our storms. This passage presents and pinpoints the places of our reliance if we are to be storm survivors.

RELY ON HIS PROMISE

If you are going to hold on to your faith while going through your storm, you must *rely on His promise*. When Jesus said, "Let us cross over to the other side," He stated it in the aorist tense and the subjunctive mood, which means the statement was an imperative. In other words, it was not a suggestion; it was a command. It was not a proposition; it was a promise. In essence, Jesus was saying, "Come what may, we are going over to the other side." Indeed, the storms of life may come, but there is no way to go under when the Lord says, "Let's go over."

When Jesus says something, we can count on it. Sometimes when storms come, we have a tendency to forget what the Lord has promised; but if He says it, then that settles it. We must remember that life's problems do not preclude the Lord's promises. The truth is that life's problems can become our preparation for the Lord's promises.

This was certainly true in the life of Abraham. God had made Abraham a promise: "I'm going to make your seed to outnumber the stars in the heaven and the sands upon the seashore." In between the promise and the provision, however, Abraham encountered some problems: lying problems, family problems, and aging problems. It was not until he was 100 years old that he finally had a son.

Then, Abraham received a message from God—to take his only son and sacrifice him. That was a real problem; however, Abraham did not hesitate, because all of his problems had only served to prepare his faith. Abraham now realized that God could do anything. He rose early in the morning, went to the mountain, and got ready to sacrifice his son. Just before he was about to slay him, God said to Abraham, "Don't harm the boy; there is a ram in the bush." Abraham sacrificed the ram instead of Isaac and then called the place Jehovah-Jireh, a name for God meaning, "The Lord Will Provide."

For every promise, there will be problems; but if you hold on, the Lord will provide. Don't throw in the towel. Don't give up the ship. Don't wave the white flag of surrender. Hold on to the Lord's promise even when the storm is raging. Hold on even when you can't see what God is doing. If you hold on to His promise, the Lord will provide.

In 1989 a severe earthquake almost flattened Armenia. This deadly tremor killed over 30,000 people in less than four minutes. In the midst of all the confusion of the earthquake, a father rushed to his son's school. When he arrived, he discovered that the building was as flat as a pancake. Standing there looking at what was left of the school, the father remembered a promise he made to his son, "No matter what, I'll always be there for you!" Tears began to fill his eyes. It looked like a hopeless situation, but he could not take his mind off his promise.

Remembering that his son's classroom was in the back right corner of the building, the father rushed there and started digging through the rubble. As he was digging, other grieving parents arrived, clutching their hearts and crying, "My son!" "My daughter!" They tried to pull him off of what was left of the school building, saying, "It's too late!" "They're dead!" "You can't help!" "Go home!" Even a police officer and a firefighter told the father that he should go home. To everyone who tried to stop him, he asked, "Are you going to help me now?" They did not answer him, so he continued digging for his son, stone by stone. He needed to know for himself the answer to his question, "Is my boy alive, or is he dead?"

This man dug for eight hours, then 12, then 24, and then 36. Finally in the 38th hour, as he pulled back a boulder, he heard his son's voice and screamed his son's name, "ARMAND!" A voice answered him, "Dad? It's me, Dad!" Then the boy added these priceless words, "I told the other kids not to worry. I told 'em that if you were alive, you'd save me; and when you saved me, then they'd be saved. You promised that, Dad. 'No matter what,' you said, 'I'll always be there for you!' And here you are, Dad. You kept your promise!" **

No matter how bad your storm is, rely on the promise, for we have a Father who always keeps His promise.

RELY ON HIS PRESENCE

Not only must we rely on His promise, but we must also *rely on His presence*. In verse 36, Mark records, "Now when they had left the multitude, they took him along in the boat as he was and other little boats were also with him." There were many boats on the Sea of Galilee that day, but the presence of Jesus marked the difference between the disciples' boat and the other boats. All they would ever need to handle the storm was already on board—in Jesus. If they were going to make it to the other side, they would have to rely on His presence.

If you are a believer in the Lord Jesus Christ, you already have all you will ever need to handle the storms of life. When the storm begins to rage, some of us look to our external friends and family who lack the ability to effect real change in our situation. Some of us look to our internal ability, education, and know-how, only to discover that there are some storms we are not equipped to handle. Thus, it's time for us to stop looking at our external partnerships and internal prowess and fix our eyes instead on the eternal presence of Jesus in our lives. Jesus is Lord, even in the storm; He can and will handle our storms.

The writer of Hebrews quoted Jesus as saying, "I will never leave you nor forsake you" (Heb. 13:5). That word "never" is a double negative— "never, ever" is the idea. He could not state his point any stronger! In the Greek, the promise is very emphatic: *"I will never, never, never leave thee."* Kenneth Wuest renders it like this, "For He himself has said, and the statement is on record, I will not, I will not cease to sustain and uphold you." *** With Jesus on board, there is no storm that you cannot handle. His presence makes all the difference.

My sons were attending Sonoran Sky Elementary School in Glendale, Arizona. The school was about two miles from our home. Fredrick Jr. was 13, and Cedrick was 10. Every day I picked them up from school at 2:55 p.m. One day Fredrick asked me, "Daddy, when can we start walking home with our friends?" I was a little apprehensive because I knew there were some busy streets to cross. I had always picked them up, but I decided we would give it a try.

I mapped out what I thought was the safest route and told my sons that they had to walk together. I gave Fredrick instructions to watch over his brother and look both ways before crossing the street. I also told them not to talk to strangers and call me before they left the school. With all of those instructions, I still did not feel comfortable with the idea of my sons walking home from school. I realized that I was being overprotective, but they were my children.

So I came up with a plan: I arrived at their school early and parked down the street out of view. When Fredrick and Cedrick left school, I watched them walk together and never let them out of my sight. I watched them cross the busy streets. I watched Fredrick and Cedrick and every person who walked by them. I was ready at any moment to step in and deliver them from any situation. I was there all the way to make sure they were safe, but they never knew it.

You need to know that God is your Father. In your storm season, He will be right there, even though you may not see or feel His presence. You may not know it, but He is right there— ready to step in and deliver you from any situation. He will never let you out of His sight. He will never leave you nor forsake you.

Notice that the presence of Jesus does not exempt you from the storm; instead, it equips you for the storm. Having Jesus doesn't mean that you won't have to deal with some junk. Having faith doesn't mean that you won't have some frustration. Having the Savior does not mean that you won't have some storms. It has been said that "God had one Son without sin, but He has none without suffering." Jesus Himself said, "In this world you will have tribulation; but be of good cheer, for I have overcome the world" (John 16:33). His presence equips you to handle the storms of life.

It is strange to hear a believer ask, "Why me?" My answer to them is, why not you? If God is your Father, if Jesus is your Savior, and the Holy Spirit is your power, why not you? You have what it takes to conquer the storm. In order to be a storm survivor, you must rely on the presence of the Savior.

RELY ON HIS POWER

Rely on His promise, rely on His presence, and finally, *rely on His power*. Look at verse 39: "And then he arose, and rebuked the wind and said to the sea, 'Peace be still.' " That word "rebuke" is the same word Jesus uses in Mark 5 to silence demons. "Rebuke" literally means, "Sit down." When He says, "Peace be still," the translation is, "Be muzzled, or shut up." He tells the wind, "Sit down," and then he tells the sea to "shut up." Jesus said, "Sit down, and shut up," and immediately the wind and the sea obeyed.

When I discovered the meaning of that word, I knew I had heard that particular phrase before. I was about 12 years old and was talking and playing in church. My mother turned around and looked at me. I did not hear the words; I just read her lips: "Sit down, and shut up." You know what I did? I sat down and shut up! Let me tell you why: my mother had proven to me that she had the power to handle me. Mama already had shown me the repercussions of not doing what she said. So when Mama spoke, I sat down and shut up.

If you were to ask the wind and the sea why they obeyed Jesus, they would have told you that "a long time ago in creation, He showed us that He had the power to handle us." He spoke, and the wind moved across the face of the deep. He spoke, and the waters separated from the land. He had already proven that He had the power to tell the wind and the waves to sit down and shut up. Likewise, no matter what storm you may be going through, God has already proven that He has the power to tell your trouble, your trial, and your turbulence, "Sit down, and shut up!"

Notice that the power is in His word. He spoke, and the storm ceased. With just a word, the Lord can still your storm. With just a word, the Lord can turn your life around. With just a word, the Lord can bless you. With just a word, the Lord can turn your pain into praise because the power is in His word.

Perhaps the disciples were living in fear because they had forgotten what they had already seen Jesus do. In chapter 1 of Mark's Gospel, with just a word He cast out an unclean spirit, and with just a word He healed a leper. In chapter 2, with just a word He healed a man who was paralyzed; and in chapter 3, with just a word He healed a man with a withered hand. By the time they got to chapter 4, they should have known that Jesus could handle a storm.

If you could look down the hallway of your own history, you would see what God has already demonstrated in your life. God has already proven that He can handle your storm. You can be a storm survivor if you will choose to live in faith and not in fear—faith that relies on

His promise, faith that relies on His presence, and faith that relies on
His power. ⌀

> I've been through the storm and rain, but I made it.
> I've had heartache and I've had pain, but I made it.
> I've been down to my last dime,
> But the Lord stepped in right on time.
> Hallelujah, thank you Jesus, I made it.
>
> -Unknown

* Dr. Harry Emerson Fosdick, *The Meaning of Faith* (Whitefish, Montana: Kessinger Publishing, 2007), 195.

** Jack Canfield and Mark Victor Hansen, *Chicken Soup for the Soul* (Deerfield Beach, Florida: HCI Books, 2001), 266.

*** Kenneth S. Wuest, *The New Testament: An Expanded Translation* (Grand Rapids: Eerdmans, 1961, reprinted 1994).

A Charge to Keep I Have
(1 Timothy 6:11-16)

———— ✧ ————

DR. ERIC A. JOHNSON

Greater Galilee Church
Louisville, Kentucky

When I was in my junior and senior year of high school, not only did I play football, but I also attempted to run track (because I didn't want to go to class). Believe it or not, I ran the 330 low hurdles and the mile. My track coach in Texas was an old, iron-tough, African American military veteran named Robert Daniels.* After our warm-up run of approximately two to three miles, Coach Daniels used to get on us (especially me) about our form and how we ran. He often hollered and screamed over and over and over again, "Johnson, you've got to tuck your elbows, get that head up, and count your steps. If you're going to clear the hurdles and survive the race, you're going to have to count your steps." Why in the world should I have been concerned about counting my steps when it was over 100 degrees outside, I'd been running all day, I was hot, I was tired, and it seemed as though my task, challenge, and workout was the hardest? At this point, all I was concerned about was counting the distance and the time. I really was not interested in counting my steps; I just wanted to finish the race I was supposed to run and hear the announcer say, "In first place, Eric A. Johnson!" Well, what Coach Daniels was trying to teach me at the tender age of 16 or 17 was that it's not so important the distance or the pace that we run: what's most important is how we run our race (cf. 1 Cor. 9:24ff). What's most important is that we run the race the right way—by counting our steps.

In his volume entitled *The Purpose Driven Life*, Rick Warren truthfully trumpets the tenet that "life is about three things: life is a *test*, life is a *trust*, and life is a *temporary* assignment." ** I like that because it reminds me that since I'm not going to be here forever, I've got to recognize the importance of counting my steps.

In our text, Paul—the prince of the New Testament, the New Testament theologian, the missionary-minded messenger, and the spiritual father of Timothy—writes this letter upon his release from his first Roman imprisonment (Acts 20) in Macedonia around A. D. 62. Paul closes his letter to Timothy, "his own son in the faith," by reminding him that he's got a charge to keep; and if he is going to keep his charge, he's got to count his steps.

Like Timothy, each of us need to be reminded here that life is not always about being comfortable, life isn't always about being cozy, and life isn't always about convenience. Life is about remembering that God has committed to us a charge to keep. This text has been tailored to teach us how Paul helps Timothy to grasp/gain this joyous jewel.

IT'S GOT TO BE PERSONAL

In verse 11, Paul tells Timothy, "But thou [or you]. . ." He is essentially saying, "Timothy,

- I know you're in Ephesus, one of the four great metropolises of the Roman world (Rome, Alexandria, and Antioch), but. . .
- I know you are in Ephesus where the temple of Diana is thriving, but. . .
- I know that there are heretics there, but. . .
- I know that there are at least a quarter of a million people there, but. . .
- I know emperor worship is strong there, but..."

In other words, Paul is reminding Timothy, "Remember, it's not what's going on outside that matters; it's what's going on inside." Likewise, you can't expect others to run your race for you. If it's going to be done, you've got to do it. God's got something personally for you to do, and He wants to use you where you are.

One day Little Johnny was in church school, and the teacher told him, "Little Johnny, sit down; Little Johnny, sit down; Little Johnny, sit down! If you don't sit down, I'm going to call your father." Little Johnny reluctantly sat down and mumbled, "I may be sitting down on the outside, but I'm standing up on the inside!" When the charge gets personal with us, we'll stand up on the inside; then it will show up on the outside. When the charge gets personal, we'll stand up, stop seeking a chance to leave, and allow God to use us where He has left us.

STAY/PLAY (IN) YOUR POSITION

Look at verse 11. Paul addresses Timothy as the person he is– "a man of God." (The genitive form is used here, which means, "man belonging to God.") This speaks to a vital concept that Paul is teaching his young protegé: because Timothy belongs to God, he must flee or be different (contrasting) from the false teachers and heretics. In short, Paul warns Timothy to avoid bad examples of the false Christ and aim for a better exegesis of the true Christ. Today, we also must not allow anything to cause us to live beneath our position.

My son J. R. and I love playing football. We were playing outside one day, and my neighbor's son came over to play with us. Because he had problems tackling me, every now and then I would jump or fall down so he could tackle me. After a couple of downs my five-year-old son J. R. walked over to me and said, "Stay (in) your position!" J. R. is radically right: if we don't want to get tackled, we'd better "stay (in) our position"! There are some things that our position won't allow:

- We are not supposed to love false teaching (v. 3). Stay (in) your position!

- We are not to be conceited, lacking in genuine spiritual knowledge, caught up in word battles and in constant friction (vv. 4-5). Stay (in) your position!
- We are to avoid heathen heresies and hedonism (v. 5b). Stay (in) your position!
- We are not to be muddied by materialism (vv. 6-10). Stay (in) your position!

Rather, we are to aim or constantly strive for these things:

- Upright conduct (v. 11);
- Open and obedient relationship with God (v. 11);
- Endurance and gentleness (v. 11);
- Trust (v. 12); and
- Goodwill toward others (v. 12).

In the words of the old Negro spiritual, "I ain't gonna let nobody, nothing turn me around. . ."

A STIRRING PATTERN OF STRUGGLE

Look at the continuous nature of Paul's words in verse 12: "Fight the good fight of faith." Paul uses the present tense of the verb to help us see that it's not only a continuous action, but it's a continuous struggle as well. The apostle is basically telling Timothy that the Christian life is a contest requiring great purpose and discipline and doing ministry in any place is a struggle. Yet, Paul says to struggle and strain with the hope of grasping eternal life. Here, the tense suggests that we grasp only a single time.

How could this be? Remember, I told you earlier that I used to run track in the smoldering Texas heat. There is always a point in track between the backstretch and the curve when the "monkey" begins to ride your back, and the only way to make it is to continually look forward, be disciplined, count steps, and continue forward. That's what Paul is telling Timothy: Life is not a sprint but a marathon.

Likewise, there will be times when the monkey of frustration, the monkey of anxiety, the monkey of disappointment, the monkey of unpaid bills, the monkey of weariness, the monkey of loneliness, and the monkey of heartbreak will get on your back. Don't quit, but fight. Keep fighting the good fight of faith, look forward (unto Jesus, the author and finisher of our faith [Hebrews 12:2]) and lay hold onto eternal life. You're not working to be saved; you're working because you are saved. Claim your calling.

Paul tells Timothy to persevere in keeping this commandment because of God's gracious display of mercy. He also tells him that God is his source and protection, his life and his stamina. Therefore, Paul urges him: "Timothy, you've got to hang in there, but not just any kind of way. You've got to do it without spot or blame." Paul wants Timothy to be able to say, "There is no shame in my game."

A DETERMINED PLEDGE OF SERVICE

Moreover, the apostle instructs Timothy that he can look to Jesus, who witnessed a good confession before Pilate. Luke 23:4 tells us that Jesus' service to His Father was so pleasing that Pilate said, "I find no fault in him." Paul encourages Timothy to serve and keep on serving until Jesus' return. He essentially tells him that if he is going to keep this serving pledge, he must remember who Jesus is and what Jesus will be.

Paul closes this portion of the letter in verses 15 and 16 with a glorious doxology that praises God for giving His servants staying power to keep their serving pledge, for being sovereign (v. 15), for His self-existence (v. 16), and for that fact that even when we feel like retreating, God encourages us to go forward.

I close with this story told by Dr. Manuel Scott Sr., the well-known Texas pastor and theologian. In a certain war, a battle was getting fierce, and the commanding officer noticed that the casualties were quickly mounting. He turned to the young bugle boy and ordered him to play the retreat song immediately. Several minutes passed, and the commanding officer again advised the bugle boy to blow his horn and sound the retreat song, yet the bugle boy still did not play. Finally, the commanding officer cried, "Bugle boy, we are losing the war! I told you to play the retreat song." The young and scared bugle boy looked at the commanding officer with a tear-stained face and said, "Sir, you know that I have done everything you ever asked me. . .I woke the soldiers up; I called them to breakfast, lunch, and dinner. Whenever you gave a command, I followed it completely; but, you see, I cannot play the retreat song because my master never taught me to play the retreat song."

God has never told the Christian soldier to retreat. God has never told the church to retreat; rather, our charge is, "Onward, Christian soldiers, marching as to war/ With the cross of Jesus going on before." *** If we do anything, let it be to go forward.

- Go forward and make it personal…
- Go forward and stay your position…
- Go forward with a stirring pattern of struggle…
- Go forward with a determined pledge of service…

As Christians, we need to say with the hymnwriter:

> A charge to keep I have,
> A God to glorify,
> Who gave His son my soul to save,
> And fit it for the sky.
>
> To serve this present age
> My calling to fulfill,
> O may it all my powers engage
> To do my Master's will. ****

* Coach Daniels never shared with me that he had been in military service, yet everyone who knew him supposed that he had been in the service because of his iron- tough, bull-dog, military temperament

** Rick Warren, *The Purpose Driven Life* (Grand Rapids: Zondervan, 2002), 42.

*** Sabine Baring-Gould and Arthur S. Sullivan, "Onward Christian Soldiers" in *The New National Baptist Hymnal* (Nashville: National Baptist Publishing Board, 1987), 385.

****Charles Wesley and Lowell Mason, "A Charge to Keep I Have" in *The New National Baptist Hymnal* (Nashville: National Baptist Publishing Board, 1987), 190.

It's Not Over…Until God Says It's Over
(John 11:1-45)

—⚬∿⚬—

MINISTER JEWEL M. LONDON

Houston, Texas

While scanning my bookshelf, my eye caught a glimpse of a little book, hidden and barely noticeable. Intrigued by the title, I pulled out *Embraced By the Light* and began to read it. This book had been a part of my collection for quite some time, yet I had never read it. As a matter of fact, I couldn't remember where it came from or who could have possibly given it to me.

This book sold over six million copies and was listed in the #1 position on the *New York Times* bestseller list for well over a year. Yet what is so significant is the storyline about a 31-year-old woman named Betty J. Eadie—a full-blooded Sioux-Indian woman's daughter raised on an Indian reservation in South Dakota, the wife of a successful white Air Force officer, and a mother of six. After surviving a neglected childhood, the divorce of her parents, and her own divorce to her *first* husband, she worked hard with her *new* husband to achieve the kind of family life she had so longed for. But one day, her imperfect yet ideal life was interrupted. . . .

After having so many children, Betty, an otherwise healthy woman, began to have medical problems and entered into the hospital to undergo a routine surgery—a partial hysterectomy. She hemorrhaged during the surgery. but the doctors were able to get it under control. Yet later that night, Betty had complications, and the massive bleeding returned. Left alone and unattended during the nurses' shift change, Betty slipped in and out of consciousness. By the time the staff returned, she was *dead.**

Her life was gone and with it all her dreams, hopes, and aspirations. What would happen now to the family she had worked so hard for? Who would help her beloved husband raise their six children?

AFRAID OF DEATH? JESUS CONQUERED IT!

Death—a very strong word—signifies the permanent cessation of life, vitality, and functionality; it is the absence of mobility, heartbeat, respiration, and consciousness. *Death*: the deprivation of existence and ultimate extinction; the reality of irreversible termination of time and purpose; the end of all things and the beginning of none.

Death. The mere mention of the word brings about thoughts of our own temporal humanity, vulnerability, and our certainty of no longer existing on the earth. For the Word of God says, "Man who is born of a woman is of few days and full of trouble" (Job 14:1 NKJV), and "...for dust thou art, and unto dust shalt thou return" (Gen. 3:19 KJV).

If you were anything like me as a kid, you probably grew up with a fear of death and anxious thoughts about how you would leave this earth, never to return. You were probably forced to attend funerals and experienced your own reactions. You also watched the reactions of others stricken with the grief, suffering, and sorrow from losing a loved one, such as weeping and wailing, falling over caskets, desiring to bring back someone who will never return—thus further intensifying your fear of death.

If the truth be told, some of us are still afraid of death. We're so afraid that we've fallen victim to the bondage and burden of the unknown, creating for ourselves quite a predicament. We experience feelings of anxiety over the cessation of our own lives, thus restraining and subjecting ourselves to a force that robs, steals, and kills our peace and tranquility.

But we can stand encouraged today. Jesus conquered this pseudo force. He said, "I am he that liveth, and was dead; and, behold, I am alive forevermore, Amen; and have the keys of hell and of death" (Rev. 1:18 KJV).

He said, ". . .Death is swallowed up in victory. O death, where is thy sting? O grave, where is thy victory? . . .But thanks be to God, which giveth us the victory through our Lord Jesus Christ" (1 Cor. 15: 54-55, 57).

In every situation, we must realize—no matter how daunting, overwhelming, challenging, frustrating, scary, or tragic our situation appears to be—"it ain't over until God says it's over." Through every struggle, God reveals how sovereign He is, how weak we are, and how our lives are changed through the process.

LORD, IF YOU HAD BEEN HERE. . .

We know the story of Lazarus because we've heard it most of our Christian lives. He fell ill due to an unknown sickness, leaving his sisters Mary and Martha in an unimaginable predicament from which there was no clear or easy way out. We don't know why he was sick, but we do know he was sick enough to call on the name of Jesus. Mary and Martha knew Benadryl couldn't cure it, Tylenol wouldn't heal it, and cortisone wouldn't take the pain away. They sent word to the one and only logical solution, Jesus Christ, to come and make everything all right: the same Jesus who turned water into wine, healed the lame, and fed the five thousand. Jesus—the one who walked on water, cast out demons, touched the blind, and gave them sight to see—was nowhere to be found. The One who could have done something didn't. When they sent word to Jesus, Lazarus was only sick, but now bad had turned to worse: he was *dead*.

Can you relate to Mary and Martha? Surely you can. For that which you knew He had the power to save, He didn't. You prayed and you hoped, you hoped and you prayed, but to no avail.

We find ourselves saying the same words Mary and Martha said: "Lord, if You had been here, my brother would not have died." We lament, "Lord, if You had been here, I wouldn't have lost my home, lost my job, lost my spouse, etc. Lord, if You had only been here. . ."

Our hearts challenge our minds, our minds challenge our spirit, and our spirit challenges our faith; so we want to ask, we dare to ask, we're afraid to ask . . "Why? Why weren't You there when I needed You the most? Why couldn't the outcome have been different? If You love me as much as You say You do, if You are truly Lord and Savior of my life, if You are God. . . Why??!!!! Why weren't You there when I needed You the most? Lord, if You had only been there. . ." Just like Martha, we too believed Jesus *could have* done something had He only made Himself available to do so.

However, God's choice to refrain from moving when we think He should move reveals His sovereignty. Even from the beginning of the passage, Jesus told His disciples, "This sickness is not unto death, but for the glory of God, that the Son of God might be glorified thereby" (John 11:4).

God knows your pain. He knows your sorrow. He even knows the grief you endure; nevertheless, that which you are experiencing is not just for you, but for the glory of God. Through your pain, God's greatness is revealed. Through your suffering, His presence is magnified. God is not unmerciful or uncaring; He is sovereign. When we honor Him in His rightful place, we affirm His right to govern the universe as He sees fit, and that includes us. He knows which hardship or trial to entrust to each individual. He knows you will ultimately be able to take the struggle in stride and yield to His perfect work through His pruning process. The psalmist said, "It was good for me that I have been afflicted; that I may learn thy statutes" (Ps. 119:71). God knows that even through your most tragic circumstance, you will learn to trust Him.

SURRENDER TO GOD, AND SEE HIS GLORY REVEALED

Incidentally, Martha experienced this very thing. Though weakened in her faith and spirit, Martha released control and surrendered to her Savior, declaring with confidence, "But I know that even now God will give you whatever you ask" (v. 22 NIV). There comes a point in time during our struggle when we have to concede to the divine will of God. It is at this point that God will remove our surface-level faith and replace it with deep faith—the kind of faith in which we still believe God is still God, even when things don't turn out the way we think they should. This is where He wants us: totally yielded and surrendered, giving Him *carte blanche* (ultimate liberty) to reveal His glory. Believe it or not, this is true liberty.

At this point, Jesus tells Martha, "Thy brother shall rise again" (v. 23). Enough said. Whenever Jesus speaks, action ALWAYS follows. Isaiah 55:11 says, "So shall my word be that goeth forth out of my mouth: it shall not return unto me void, but it shall accomplish that which I please, and it shall prosper in the thing whereto I sent it." There is no room for discussion when the Word has been spoken.

Anguished in His spirit over the sorrow of those in pain, Jesus delayed their relief no longer. I thank God for a Savior who is not without emotion, compassion, or concern. When we suffer, He suffers. When we hurt, He hurts. He has endured all that we have endured and more.

We know how the story ends: Jesus tells the spectators to take away the stone. Martha allows doubt to challenge her faith and, in turn, challenges

Jesus ("By this time he stinketh" [v. 39]). As the awesome Savior that He is, Jesus gently rebuked yet encouraged Martha and said, "Did I not tell you that if you believed, you would see the glory of God?" (v. 40 NIV).

He calls Lazarus forth, raises him from the dead, and releases him from his grave clothes. He calls "life out of death," not for His sake, but for the glory of God—for those around Him so they might truly know He was sent by the Father.

Martha understood that the resurrection would take place on the last day, but Jesus wanted her to understand that all power was in His hands. She didn't have to wait until the last day; she could have her victory today. Jesus told Martha, "I am the resurrection and the life. He who believes in me will live…" (v. 25 NIV).

Lazarus' resurrection was of no surprise to Jesus because the end was determined before the beginning. God's sovereignty was revealed, the weakness of man's faith was exposed, and now lives were changed for His glory: "Therefore many of the Jews who had come to visit Mary, and had seen what Jesus did, put their faith in Him" (v. 45 NIV).

PUSHING PAST SURFACE-LEVEL FAITH

Will you allow the sovereignty of God to deliver others through your challenges? Will you push past surface-level faith and surrender to a deeper faith? Can you believe God beyond your limited perception? Though your dreams *appear* to be dead and life seems far beyond your comprehension, will you believe Jesus can, will, and wants to do what He says He can do?

He is the resurrection and the life. This means that He can make *whatever* you lost, *whatever* slipped through your fingers, *whatever* lay limp and lifeless live again! It means that He can take spiritual existence, transcend physical death, and return vitality to your unhappy soul. In Him is life—*another* chance, *another* opportunity, to live and live more abundantly (John 10:10).

In the beginning, I told you the story of Betty J. Eadie's death. What I didn't tell you is that she didn't stay dead. She had what is known as a NDE, or near death experience. Betty had been dead for at least four hours and was classified as clinically dead—no life, no breath, no vitality. Yet during that time, she went on a journey; she went to have a little talk with Jesus. Jesus told Betty that she died prematurely and to go back because she hadn't completed her mission on earth. In obedience, she returned.

I was curious to find out what happened to Betty, so I did a little research and found her on the Internet.** Within the past 30-plus years since her NDE, Betty has been volunteering her time with dying patients and their families, traveling extensively throughout the United States, Canada, and Great Britain, writing and speaking on death and what awaits us beyond *this* life, and planning the release of a movie. Moreover, she is offering relevant information, not only about experiencing the afterlife with God, but also about living this life in a fulfilling way. Today, Betty and her husband celebrate over their 44 years of marriage, their eight children, their 16 grandchildren, and their three great-grandchildren.

Before Betty died, she had lived life on her own terms. Today, she lives her life based on the mandates of Jesus. I have to believe that Lazarus' resurrection was similar to Betty's—that God allowed him to return because his mission had not been completed. His life was used for the glory of God because it caused others to believe.

Jeremiah 29:11 (NIV) says, " 'For I know the plans I have for you,' declares the Lord, 'plans to prosper you and not to harm you, plans to give you hope and a future.' " Your yesterdays are gone, and your tomorrows lay ahead. Yes, challenges and circumstances have weakened your faith; but push past them, and hold fast to your faith. Make a choice today. BELIEVE again. Remember, it's not over until God says it's over. ∽

* Betty J. Eadie, *Embraced By the Light* (Detroit: Gold Leaf Press, 1992).

** Embraced by the Light website – http://embracedbythelight.com

Preaching with a Problem
(2 Corinthians 12:7-10)

———∞———

REV. DR. AARON MCNAIR SR.

Mt. Moriah Community Church
Raleigh, North Carolina

New Mt. Moriah Community Church
Farmville, North Carolina

The preaching of the gospel is the most important occupation any person can be called to do, but it also ranks as one of the highest-stress level jobs in existence. Medical doctors have concluded that one hour of preaching (Pentecostal-style) is equivalent to eight hours of daily labor.

Although it is the most important occupation in the world, preaching is also a highly criticized one. Persons who have been preachers of the gospel for any length of time bear witness that this is a job in which you must endure persecution, envy, strife, jealousy, and stigmatizing. Seemingly, the preacher is always under the eye of scrutiny.

With all of the problems mentioned and those which are not, the preacher must never back down from what God has called, hired, appointed, and anointed him to do. Although the preacher should always be respected and cared for, he should never be the focal point of his own ministry. Instead, the preacher's focus should be on souls who are in need of this glorious gospel we are allowed to preach. This is the preacher's motivation—that he has a message to deliver straight from his heart to the hearer's very soul.

DESPITE RESISTANCE AND LACK OF TIME—PREACH!

Sometimes, the biggest problem the preacher has involves speaking to a congregation he knows doesn't want to change. So, preachers deliver their sermons with a hope that the power of the gospel will create a change—even in unexpected places and people. Sometimes it does, as it did in the wicked city of Nineveh after a preacher by the name of Jonah delivered a powerful, unnamed sermon. (The governor on down to the ordinary people repented.) But from that same Bible, we also find the sad story of a preacher named Noah who preached daily to a people refusing to change. Despite not seeing any change, the preacher kept on giving the same sermon. Both preachers had a problem, yet they kept on preaching.

Actually, every preacher will always testify that he is preaching with a problem amidst his faithful study of the Word of God, as well as his reading of good books to help produce rich sermons and laying before the Lord to get a word.

As Protestant preachers, we are not as fortunate as the Roman Catholic, Episcopal, and Lutheran denominations that have weekly sermons prepared for them. Instead, we must allow the guidance of the Holy Spirit to be paramount in our sermon preparation. Thus, *time* often becomes a problem for some preachers, particularly the bi-vocational ones. We are always preaching with a problem!

DESPITE YOUR PAST AND PHYSICAL PROBLEMS—PREACH!

From our text we read about this energetic, commanding, masterful man who is one of the greatest characters in the Bible and history—*the apostle Paul*. Yes, the chief missionary had been a persecutor of Christ and of Christians.

Enthusiastically, Paul had endeavored to stamp out the Christian faith. In fact, he was standing there when they stoned Deacon Stephen to death. But on the Damascus road, the persecutor became a believer. (Some of the problems that Paul encountered resulted from his past. You may not realize that some folks will never forget what you used to be. However, God doesn't consult your past to determine your future.) In spite of it all, Paul became a great missionary and church builder and undertook three fruitful missionary journeys. In all of his travels, trials, and triumphs, Paul was borne along by one incentive: "to do the will of Him that sent me."

Paul was a heart-stirring preacher despite his problems. Three of the apostle's sermons are preserved for us in the Book of Acts and serve as models for preachers for all time. He relied upon the Old Testament Scriptures, often referring to their historical facts and prophecies to make his point. When you ponder his sermon to the Jews at Antioch and the one he delivered to the Gentiles at Athens, you can see that Paul was considerate of the people's needs—spiritual, physical, mental, and moral. In the same way, today's preachers should always shoot for the heart and not the feet.

Paul was the most gifted writer of the 27 books that make up the New Testament. He was the author of 14 of them, if you include the Book of Hebrews.

Along with his other problems, Paul's bodily size and appearance may have been a mark against him. Little in stature and partly bald, he also had crooked legs, eyes set close together, and a hooked nose. But in spite of his physical deformities, Paul lived only to win others to Christ and make Him known.

DESPITE YOUR THORN IN THE FLESH—PREACH!

In our text we read that Paul, like preachers today, had received great revelations. As preachers, we must remember that all of our revelation knowledge is a gift from God. Paul was tempted to become conceited in light of his great revelations. To keep that from happening, God sent him a thorn in his flesh. This expression—similar to the Septuagint terminology, "thorn in the side"—was a metaphorical description of trouble inflicted by God.

It is difficult to know precisely what the apostle had in mind. He also called this thorn a messenger of Satan that brought him torment, but he said nothing else. Several things could have been meant by "a thorn in the flesh." First, Paul had a physical ailment, according to Galatians 4:15. He could have had an eye disease or a speech impediment. Second, Paul spoke of continuing opposition *in* the church. Finally, he pointed to some troubling demonic activity, perhaps some severe temptations.

Despite this uncertainty, Paul's main idea is clear. He asked God three times to remove this thorn from his life to help him to be more effective in ministry. Yet God told him that divine grace was sufficient for him. The tense of the expression he used may also be translated as *"He has said,"* indicating that Paul regarded God's statement as more than one simply directed toward his present situation. God wanted Paul to find comfort and security in the grace he had received in Christ—the same thing God desires for all believers.

In fact, in this particular case, God's denial of Paul's request turned out to be for Paul's greater good because it was for God's greater glory. God told Paul that divine power is made perfect in weakness. Throughout the Scriptures, God delights in displaying His power in situations where human strength is weak (1 Sam. 14:6-15). When God's people are weak, then God's strength becomes evident.

As a result, Paul determined that he would boast all the more gladly about his weakness. He quit complaining so that Christ's power might rest on him. The terminology translated "rest" (*episkenoo*) may be translated as "to tabernacle" or "pitch a tent." It is likely that Paul drew upon Old Testament imagery of the glory of God coming upon the tabernacle (Exod. 40:34-38). If so, he learned that taking delight in his thorn actually brought God's glory to his ministry and preaching. From this understanding, Paul concluded that he would rather delight in his weaknesses than harbor resentment about them.

Paul had to suffer imprisonment and continuous exposure to death. (He received 39 lashes five times, was beaten with rods three times, and was shipwrecked three times.) He often suffered from cold and hunger, and his life was constantly in danger from bandits, Jews, and Gentiles. But most of all, Paul made it known that he suffered the most within himself because of the sorry condition of the church.

All of this could be classified as elements of Paul's thorn. Paul said he begged the Lord to take it away. Nevertheless, each time the Lord kept telling Paul, "My grace is sufficient for thee," which means, "My favor is all you need." (In other words, "So what if you got problems, as long as I keep blessing you!") God was telling Paul, "I know you feel weak from your troubles, but My power works best in your weakness." After Paul heard this, he was encouraged and said, "Well, since I know it is all for Christ's good, I am content with my thorn—with all my weakness, insults, hardships, persecution, and calamities. For when I am weak, then I am strong."

- When they lie about you, it hurts (yet He's going to bless you!), but it makes you stronger—preach!
- When they pull against your vision, it hurts, but it makes you stronger—preach!
- When they refuse to support you, it hurts, but it makes you stronger—preach!
- When you're afflicted, it hurts, but it makes you stronger—preach!

- When you're tired, it hurts, but it makes you stronger—preach!

- When you're hurt, it makes you stronger—preach!

- When nobody understands you, it hurts, but it makes you stronger—preach!

- When you feel like throwing in the towel—preach!

When you feel like you are weak, that's a good time to preach, because Paul said that's when you're at your best. That's when you are strongest—when you find yourself preaching with (and in spite of) your problems:

- *Moses had a problem with inadequacy.* He felt like he did not have what it took to be effective. All he had was his walking stick, because he was old, along with his stuttering problem. But God told him, "Take your stick and your stutter and go!"

- *Jonah had a problem with bitterness, fear, and resentment.* He went through hell but discovered that he still had to preach with his problems.

- *The Samaritan woman had a problem with lost dignity and respect.* Yet she had to go back and preach to a city where she had no favor, "Come see a man!"

- *Priscilla's problem was that she lived in a time when women were ordered to be quiet and Christians were persecuted.* But in spite of her problems, she preached!

- *Paul had problems down in Athens; they told him he wasn't anything and counted him as nothing but a babbler.* But Paul kept on preaching about an unknown God!

- *Hosea had a problem named Gomer, the prostitute.* But he still prophesied to the Israelites.

- *Jesus had His problems; they called Him a devil.* But He still preached about the kingdom of God.

Jeremiah summed it all up. First, he had a problem with his age: he felt like he would be despised for his youth. Then he had a problem with God; he was upset because he felt like God didn't hold up to His end of the prophecy. Jeremiah was being ridiculed, so he said, "That's it! I've got a problem! No longer will I even mention His name; no longer will I speak in His name. Yet His word is like a burning fire shut up in my bones, and it's making me weary. In spite of my problems I've got to preach, lest I die!" As preachers today, each one of us is compelled to say,

- I've got to tell the sick that there is a balm in Gilead.
- I've got to tell the sinners that the wages of sin is death, but there is an escape from death.
- I've got to tell the backsliders that God is a God of second chances.
- I've got to tell the saints about prosperity and all of their inheritance.

The apostle Paul said, "Woe, woe, woe, unto me if I preach not this glorious gospel (1 Cor. 9:16). He also declared, "Oh, how beautiful are the feet of those who preach the gospel" (Rom. 10:15, cf. Isa. 52:7).

Paul told his young apprentice Timothy, "I have fought a good fight and I have kept the faith. Now the only thing I see is a crown for me" (2 Tim. 4:7-8). Well, I just want to encourage you to fight on:

- Your steps may be getting slow, but that's all right. Fight on!
- Your voice may not be as strong as it used to be, but that's all right. Fight on!
- You may not be able to do in this season of your life what you did in the other seasons of your life, but that's all right. Fight on! ✍

God Will Not Accept "No" For Your Answer
(Jonah 1)

———∽———

REVEREND BREONUS M. MITCHELL SR.

Greater Grace Temple Community Church
Nashville, Tennessee

Incumbent with the acceptance of Jesus Christ as our personal Lord and Savior is the acknowledgement and acceptance of His calling on our lives. This principle is foundational to our faith, so it is imperative that we grasp it. The primary reason for this is that even though God has a destiny for our lives, this destiny is often predicated on our ability to fully understand the duty God has for us to fulfill.

Herein often lies the struggle most of us believers have when we are reconsidering our faith and faithfulness. Often, the reason we struggle with completely making Christ the first priority and center of our life is because we struggle with submitting completely to the assignment that God wants us to accomplish. Like Jonah, you and I have been given an assignment.

This prophetic book opens with this assignment as the central part of the narrative. God's assignment for Jonah is to "go at once to Nineveh, that great city, and cry out against it; for their wickedness has come up before me" (v. 2 NRSV). God assigns Jonah a place to attend to—Nineveh. God assigns Jonah to a people to whom he would appeal—the Assyrians. God assigns Jonah to a purpose to address—their wickedness.

God has a place for us to attend, a people for us to appeal to, and a purpose for us to address. God has a specific place for us to serve in ministry. God has a specific people we have been assigned to reach. Moreover, God has a specific purpose or need that must be addressed. Yet, the reality is that most, if not all of us, tend to spend a majority of our lives debating, deviating, denying, detesting, and disobeying the assignment that God has given to us. In spite of this, just like Jonah, we often discover that God does not accept "no" for our answer.

Be reminded that Jonah was the only biblical prophet who ran away *before* delivering his message; all other Old Testament prophets ran *after* giving their messages. Also, Jonah was the only prophet who ran away *from* his message; the others ran away *because* of their messages. In fact, Jonah earned a place in the most-read book in the entire world not because of his obedience, but rather because of his disobedience. Had Jonah obeyed the voice of God, it is possible that we may never have known his name.

Thus, much—if not most—of the Book of Jonah is a pragmatic narrative on the consequences of debating, deviating, denying, detesting, and disobeying God's assignment for our lives. Again, like Jonah, it is an assignment for which God will not accept "no" for our answer.

The specifics of the assignment are these: Jonah is ordered to go into a foreign and adversarial country, Nineveh, the heart and capital of the Assyrian empire, and pronounce God's disgust with their disgraceful behavior. It would be like us going to North Korea or Tehran and pronouncing judgment in the name of Jesus Christ. Jonah was to "go at once to Nineveh, that great city, and cry out against it; for their wickedness has come up before me" (1:2 NRSV).

Granted, Jonah's defense for his disobedience is well noted and must be considered. He doesn't offer the poor and petty excuses we give for not obeying or submitting to our assignment. He hasn't the excuse of a common cold, convenient amnesia, or opportune fatigue. Jonah's disobedience is not entirely illogical.

Yet Jonah's defense is not presented to us until the end of the book; however, for the sake of introduction, it is necessary to state that defense here: "Jonah prayed to the Lord and said, 'Please Lord, was not this what I said while I was still in my own country? Therefore, in order to forestall this I fled to Tarshish, for I knew that Thou art a gracious and compassionate God, slow to anger and abundant in lovingkindness, and one who relents concerning calamity' " (4:2 NAS). Jonah defends his disobedience by declaring that this assignment has no contingencies. There is no message pertaining to the result or conclusion, and there are no finalities. There is no "if you can find one righteous person" condition (as in the case of Lot) with this assignment. The last word is with God—a God who is "gracious and compassionate, slow to anger and abounding in lovingkindness" (Ps. 103:8). Jonah has been given the assignment to tell the enemy that they have a chance to turn their situation around. For this rebellious prophet, the possibility and potentiality that God may bless the enemy makes it difficult to say "yes" to his assignment. So, to this command, Jonah emphatically responds, "No."

Now, Jonah is not some lonely creature afar off in the ages somewhere, having an experience that is unique and incommunicable. The experience of Jonah is that of every believer, not only because of his disobedience, but due to the reality that most, if not all of us, have an issue when—like Jonah—our assignment has the likelihood of blessing and benefiting our enemy.

As a result, Jonah is headed in the opposite direction, contradicting the assignment that he has been given. He is still a prophet, but he is a prophet out of place. This is a blatant reminder that in our lives we can have a religious career without truly accomplishing our righteous calling. In other words, it suggests that it is possible to take our gifts in the wrong direction. It also says to us that the even greater struggle with our assignment involves our complete lack of control of who the beneficiaries will be. This speaks directly to us in a "name-it-and-claim-it, believe-it-and-receive-it, blab-it-and-grab-it, call-it-and-haul it" world about the reality that God doesn't always leave the endings and effects up to us. He can bless whomever He wants—whenever He wants, wherever He wants, and however He wants—simply because He is God. In fact, the reason most of us possess what we possess is due to the fact that God has the last word.

Jonah is a prophet who learns that God does not permit us at times to debate, deviate from, deny, detest, or disobey His assignment for our lives. He is a prophet who discovers that God does not accept "no" for an answer. What are the lessons we can learn from Jonah when we debate, deviate from, deny, detest, or disobey our assignment?

DISOBEDIENCE LEADS TO A DISTORTED PERSPECTIVE

God gives Jonah the assignment: "Arise, go to Nineveh the great city and cry against it, for their wickedness has come up before Me" (1:2 NAS). Notice Jonah's response and reaction: "But Jonah rose up to flee to Tarshish from the presence of the Lord. So he went down to Joppa, found a ship which was going to Tarshish, paid the fare and went down into it to go with them to Tarshish from the presence of the Lord" (1:3). If there ever is a picture of how disobedience can lead to a distorted perspective, it is found here. The narrative consistently puts before us Jonah's intent and distorted perspective—"to flee from the presence of the Lord."

Jonah's distorted perspective results in his attempt to escape a spiritual assignment by relocating geographically. Jonah contended that if he fled to a place where no fellow believers could be found, this would ensure that God's word would not come to him again. Disobedience distorts our perspective and can deceive us into thinking that if we could just move to another side of town or another city and/or state, then we can escape our assignment. We may also tell ourselves that if we joined another church, changed our major, found another career, or got a new hook-up, it would enable us to escape our assignment. Have we forgotten the words of the psalmist who said, "Where can I go from your spirit? Or where can I flee from your presence? If I ascend to heaven, you are there; if I make my bed in Sheol, you are there. If I take the wings of the morning and settle at the farthest limits of the sea, even there your hand shall lead me, and your right hand shall hold me fast" (Psalm 139:7-10 NRSV). When God has an assignment for you, it will find you—wherever you try to hide.

Also, Jonah shows a distorted perspective by thinking that he can escape a spiritual assignment because his resources are great. The original language suggests that when Jonah got to Joppa, he did not just buy a ticket to Tarshish but the boat as well. This is a reminder to those of us who think that we can either buy our way out of our assignment or, because of our financial status, we do not have to accept our assignment. Like Jonah, we discover that even though we may have the resources to buy the boat, it is God who still owns the water. Whenever we think that we can buy our way out of our assignment, we end up like Jonah: we get more than what we paid for.

Once again, Jonah's distorted perspective shows itself when he thinks he has escaped his spiritual assignment because of the results he has been given. (Isn't it crazy how circumstances can become favorable, even when we are headed in the wrong direction?) What is the likelihood that Jonah would get to Joppa and find a boat headed in the opposite direction, as well as having the resources to buy the boat and crew?

Disobedience can also make us misconstrue circumstances. We tend to think that because we got the gig, the promotion, the engagement, or the appointment, it justifies our position and perspective. What Jonah does not understand is that even though it appears everything is working in his favor, he is actually headed in one direction—*down*. He goes *down* to Joppa, *down* to the bottom of the ship, *down* into the ocean, and *down* into the belly of a great whale.

DISOBEDIENCE LEADS TO DANGEROUS PREDICAMENTS

The text states, "But the Lord hurled a great wind upon the sea, and such a mighty storm came upon the sea that the ship threatened to break up" (1:4 NRSV). God, who has appeared passive, unconcerned, and inactive until now, intervenes. Like Tom Glavin throwing a strike or Donovan McNabb throwing downfield for a touchdown, God throws down a strong wind on the sea. What is God saying? He is saying that He will not be brushed aside or ignored. The silence of God does not mean that He is sightless. God is always watching, and in His time He will intervene.

This is a dangerous predicament for Jonah because his disobedience injures the innocent. Jonah is not the only victim of his disobedience; it is also the crew. Listen to the words of the text: "Then the mariners were afraid, and each cried to his god. They threw the cargo that was in the ship into the sea, to lighten it for them" (1:5 NRSV). We need to understand that disobeying the assignment God has for us affects all those connected relationally to us: marriages fail, children are injured, homes are destroyed, congregations go under, ministries function beneath their potential, sickness increases, crime intensifies, and drugs imprison others. How many "others" have been injured and wounded because of our personal disobedience? It is a fact that our disobedience injures the innocent.

Also, this is a dangerous predicament because Jonah's disobedience inoculates his intentions. The boat is now in the hands of an angry God. Even though it is not their fault, these sailors do the best they can to handle the situation. All they know to do is to lighten the load of the ship. God is throwing a storm, so the sailors throw boxes off the ship. Now, before we are quick to laugh at the efforts of these sailors, we should do some self-evaluation. How many times in our lives have we made a human stab to address what is a heavenly problem? How do we handle life when God is the problem? Do we try to calm the storm by throwing out boxes of appointments, associations, and agendas? God is throwing a storm, so the sailors throw boxes. Yet every good attempt to resolve the situation and save the ship is to no avail. Likewise, when we are disobedient, God inoculates our intentions because, as pointed out in the text, it is never about our skills; instead, it is about God's will.

Moreover, this is a dangerous predicament because Jonah's disobedience finally identifies the invisible. God is throwing a storm, so the sailors are throwing cargo. The obvious question is, "Where is Jonah?" Jonah is asleep, lying in the corner of the hold below the tormented and troubled deck. Isn't it amazing that the same rocking boat that troubles the sailors simply rocks Jonah to sleep? The text states, "Jonah, meanwhile, had gone down into the hold of the ship and had lain down and was fast asleep" (1:5 NRSV).

Jonah's sleep indicates how persons who are disobedient can be delusional and in denial about their respective situations. The alcoholic is never convinced that alcohol is the issue. The drug addict is never convinced that drugs are the issue. The Christian is never convinced that unforgiveness or faithlessness is the issue. They are all sleeping while everything around them is breaking up.

However, eventually what Jonah thinks is invisible becomes identifiable. The captain came and said to him, "What are you doing sound asleep? Get up, call on your god! Perhaps the god will spare us a thought so that we do not perish" (1:6 NRSV). Jonah cannot hide anymore. His disobedience can no longer be hidden. God does speak to Jonah; but this time it is not in private, as on dry land. This time it is in public—on the sea, from a captain.

Perhaps it is here that we need to understand that God cannot be confined to nationalities and denominations—or countries and styles of worship. God can speak wherever, whenever, and however. These aren't the captain's words! This is *God* speaking to Jonah through the captain: "What are you doing sound asleep?"

Yet it is the request of the captain that incriminates Jonah. The captain tells Jonah, "Get up, call on your god!" He asks Jonah to do what he is not in a position to do: pray. It is a dangerous predicament to be in a position where you can't use your gifts because of your own guilt. How do you handle life when your anointing is needed but your character is in the way?

Sadly, what Jonah has been trying to escape becomes obvious. After casting lots, the lot falls on Jonah. Jonah is now a prophet out of place. He is a prophet who learns that God does not permit us at times to debate, deviate from, deny, detest, or disobey his assignment for our lives. He is a prophet who discovers that God does not accept "no" for an answer.

DISOBEDIENCE DIRECTS US TO THE PREVIOUS

The fact is that whenever we tell God "no," life takes us on a journey. Regardless how long, enjoyable, or exciting it may be, eventually that journey ends right back where we started. Like Jonah, we are back in the presence of the God from whom we've tried to escape. However, it should be noted that the journey back to God is often never as easy as when we left.

Briefly notice the difficulty of Jonah's return to God. The question is a simple one for the sailors, "What shall we do to you, that the sea may quiet down for us?" (1:11). Jonah gives them the most incomprehensible response: "Pick me up and throw me into the sea; then the sea will quiet down for you: for I know it is because of me that this great storm has come upon you (1:12)."

Here, we see a form of disobedience—not from Jonah, but from the sailors. Instead of tossing Jonah overboard, they make a valiant attempt to get the ship back to land: "But they could not, for the sea grew more and more stormy against them" (1:13 NRSV). Perhaps this is God's word for those of us who seek to cover the ones who are functioning outside of their assignment. The word is that some things in life do not come with a "rewind" button. You must realize that some situations cannot be handled by your abilities. After several minutes of making futile and feeble attempts, the sailors come to one conclusion: they had thrown the wrong cargo overboard: "So they picked Jonah up and threw him into the sea; and the sea ceased from its raging" (1:14).

In conclusion, you and I have been given an assignment. God has a place for us to attend, a people for us to appeal to; and a purpose for us to address. We cannot attempt to debate, deviate from, deny, detest, or disobey the assignment that God has given to us. This is because God will not take "no" for an answer. Your assignment requires a response, and that response must be "yes."

I once read an old Pilgrim quote that said: "The purpose of problems is to push you toward obedience to God's laws, which are exact and cannot be changed. We have the free will to obey them or disobey them. Obedience will bring harmony, disobedience will bring more problems." Jonah's life is like an out-of-tune symphony. He is a prophet who is out of place, simply because God will not take "no" for answer.

Today, you and I must accept our assignment. We must be able to say wholeheartedly with the songwriter: ⟨⟩

> Lord, I'm available to you.
> My will I give to you; I will do what you say do
> Use me, Lord,
> To show someone the way and enable me to say,
> My storage is emptied, and I am available to you
>
> I am giving back to you,
> All the tools you gave to me
> My hands, my ears, voice, my eyes so you can use them as you please
> I am lifting up my cup so that you can fill it up
> Now I'm free, and I just want to be available to you.

Who's in Charge?
(1 Samuel 17)

———— ⌁ ————

REV. DENNIS PHELPS, PH.D.

New Orleans Baptist Theological Seminary
New Orleans, Lousiana

On August 29, 2005, everything changed—at least for metropolitan New Orleans and much of the Mississippi Gulf Coast. One word explained it: "Katrina." It had been several generations since a hurricane of such magnitude (Category 4 at landfall) visited the region with such devastation.

In the aftermath, one issue with multiple questions dominated the minds of the stranded thousands: *"Who's in control? Why aren't they helping us? Where are our leaders? Where is the New Orleans mayor, Ray Nagin? Where is the Louisiana governor, Kathleen Blanco? Where is the FEMA director, Michael Brown? Where is the Secretary of the Department of Homeland Security, Mike Chertoff? Where is the United States president, George W. Bush? Why aren't they helping us? Who's in charge?"*

Few of them understood that in the background a political battle was raging, with their safety and rescue hanging in the balance. It wasn't until a previously little-known military leader, three-star Lt. Gen. Russel Honoré, entered the picture that order began to be restored in the prevailing anarchy.

We have been there before. On March 20, 1981, a shooting outside the Washington, D. C. Hilton Hotel launched a day of confusion and drama. After delivering a speech to the Building & Construction Trades Council, President Ronald Reagan was shot by John Hinckley. Within minutes after the president was thrown by another Secret Service agent into the presidential limo and driven to George Washington University Hospital, questions began to ricochet throughout the corridors of power in our nation's capital: *"Where is Vice President Bush? Where is the Speaker of the House of Representatives? Who is in charge during this national crisis?"*

At a hastily called news conference, it was Secretary of State Alexander Haig who gripped the sides of the presidential podium and declared, *"I'm in charge here."* Of course, it wasn't long until others quickly reminded the Cabinet that the vice president was actually the appropriate one to be in charge.

For a while in the midst of a crisis, no one is sure who is actually in charge.

In 1 Samuel 17, God's people are also in crisis. In fact, they have been in crisis for many years. No longer listening to God, the religious leaders are living in disobedience and unfaithfulness. The Ark of the Covenant is lost, which causes some to conclude that God must be weak and unable to protect them. (Some of the laypersons seem to know more about prayer and relating to the Lord than the religious professionals.)

The Israelites' dream of having a leader like the other neighboring cultures has not ushered in paradise; instead, it is becoming a nightmare. As their king, Saul is a divine joke. His selection is dubious at best. (In that day, anointing oil was usually poured from a common jug rather than smearing and saturating the person with it from a ram's horn.) His life is a living parable of presenting the form of godliness but not the reality—style but not substance, form but not power, imitation but not relationship, substitution but not Spirit.

One wonders, *"Who's in charge?"*

Into this chaos we discover one of the largest and most significant sections of narrative to be found in the entire Samuel collection. The setting is a face-to-face stand-off between the army of the Philistines and the army of Israel. The parallel descriptions heighten the stark conflict of this national confrontation.

Then a specific character comes forward—a "champion" named Goliath, an Anakim from Gath. Gath is one of the five chief cities of the Philistines. We learn of Gath and the Anakim in Joshua 11:21-22 and 13:3. God instructs the Israelites to remove them from the Land of Promise, but the Israelites fail to do it. When Goliath of Gath steps forward, God's people are confronted with one of the consequences of their disobedience. He is very prepared and is described as some sort of professional fighting machine—a true *army of one*. His appearance intimidates and dares anyone to move against him. His challenge is both direct and vivid. He stands, shouts, and dares the Israelites across the Valley of Elah ("The Valley of the Tree"). He defies the people of God and challenges them to mortal combat. There is no room to underestimate this enemy.

Who will respond? Who *can* respond? Look at verse 11: The hearts of King Saul and all the men in Israel's army melt in paralyzing fear. Is Egyptian-like bondage on the horizon? Will there be any exodus from this crisis? Who will prevail?

WHO'S IN CHARGE?: GOD LOOKS ON THE HEART

Onto the stage steps a second character. He is introduced as someone with an unimpressive family background. He is the youngest of eight sons of an aging father. In fact, his presence keeps the family from remaining the theologically perfect size of seven sons. His three oldest brothers follow King Saul and serve on the front lines, but this youngest son is not in the army. He is relegated to the role of family-errand boy and shepherd in the smallest of villages. In some ways he is like Israel herself—small, overlooked, the rejected runt of the litter. He offers really nothing that would present himself as an important contributor to this event. That is all we know about him at this point. . .quite a contrast, at least, with his three oldest brothers.

Have there been times when you have felt insignificant? Left out? Overlooked? Inadequate? Have there been times when you wondered if God really knew what He was doing when He called you to serve?

But God does not look at the *externals* of our lives. Check out 1 Samuel 16:7. He had already looked past David's externals. God knows and examines *our hearts*; that is His primary interest. He does not choose to use many strong, noble, sophisticated, or impressive people to do His will. Instead, He chooses the weak, the common, the simple, the overlooked, the inadequate, the runt, and the broken.

WHO'S IN CHARGE?: THE BATTLE OF GOOD VS. EVIL

Verse 16 pulls us back into the conflict. *Terrorism strikes the community!* In fact, the intimidation has been going on for at least *40 days*, all the while preventing the men from tending to families, animals, and crops—paralyzing the community life.

David's assignment from his father is trivial within the context of such an enormous crisis. It is a menial task that is focused on the well-being of his three oldest brothers. Yet David discharges his duty faithfully and without question.

Verses 21-22 return us again to the conflict between the Philistines and Israel. Both sides take their places in battle array, army against army. David delivers his packages, scampers over to check on his brothers, and peeks at the converging action—unprepared for what is about to take place.

The Philistine "champion" again emerges and issues his challenge. God's people fearfully flee. Some of the men ask David if he has ever seen such a sight. They tell him that King Saul has offered money, pleasure, security, and status to any man who can slay Goliath. Still, Goliath's direct defiance goes unmet by the Israelites.

The tension grows. David now becomes involved in the battlefront drama and interprets the development as a spiritual crisis. He calls it a "reproach" from an "uncircumcised" (outside the covenant) Philistine against the armies "of God" (rather than armies of Israel). Do you hear the terms? Aren't they theological rather than national? David sees this as a God-issue in which unbelievers are trying to intimidate God Himself! This is a conflict of cultures, values, theologies, world views, and ultimately a conflict between gods.

I recognize that this flies in the face of post-modernity, but there is a real battle between right and wrong in our world. Good *does* exist. Evil *does* exist. Did anyone else notice that within hours of 9/11, the category of "evildoers" became an acceptable term in our culture. . .at least for a few weeks?

But our fight is not against flesh and blood; it is against the world forces of this present darkness. It is against spiritual forces of evil in the heavenlies (Eph. 6:12). Our true conflicts are *spiritual* rather than national, political, ethnic, or personal.

Conflict is present even in David's family. His brothers follow King Saul, but David follows another King. Eliab's attitude confirms why God directed Samuel to avoid anointing him from within Jesse's household. His judgment of others, even of his own brother, is flawed. Eliab and the other older brothers reject David and question his motives (just like Joseph's brothers did to him).

WHO'S IN CHARGE?: THE GOD OF THE EXODUS AND THE PARTING OF THE RED SEA

David's involvement deepens as his words reach King Saul's ears, but personal ambition does not draw him further into this conflict. David does not travel to Elah expecting to throw himself into anything. Instead, Saul has to seek out David. But once questioned, David is willing to be the representative of the "armies of the living God" and confront Goliath from Gath.

King Saul admits that David is untrained and too young, but David recalls the face of danger from the past. *That* is the basis of David's willingness. Like *faithful* Israelites remembering the deliverance acts of God, David understands God's actions in history on His people's behalf. He trusts in God *now* because of God's actions in the *past*. He believes that God will deliver him from the wild beast Goliath, just like God delivered him from the wild beasts of the field. As with the exodus from Egyptian slavery and the rescue through the Red Sea, God could be trusted *now* because He was trustworthy *then*.

Saul grants David permission and speaks a brief prayer over him. But look at verse 37. Don't his words seem *terse* in light of what is at stake and the enormity of this event? Is it possible that King Saul simply has absolutely no clue about what is taking place?

WHO'S IN CHARGE?: DIVINE ENABLEMENT VS. HUMAN DEVICES

David now prepares for the conflict with Goliath. He tries King Saul's gear but quickly rejects it. Instead, he takes his stick, sling, and some smooth stones to fight the giant. He rejects Saul's approach, identifying with previous great, godly shepherd-leaders—leaders such as Abraham, Isaac, Jacob, and Moses. He values divine enablement more than human devices.

As David leaves for the battle, we are reminded again of how *unknown* he is to "the powers that be." Look at verses 55-56. King Saul and his commander have no idea who this young man is.

The Philistine "champion" now moves forward again, anticipating the battle. His shock over seeing such a puny runt only incites more godless invective from his mouth. He is personally insulted that such a puny representative would be sent to deal with him. The giant from Gath pronounces divine curses, personal attacks, and intimidating fatal promises. He threatens to kill David, dishonor his corpse, and deny him any honorable burial. Goliath is oblivious to the fact that by cursing a son of Abraham, he is bringing down God's curse on *himself* (Gen. 12:3).

Now we hear the longest dialogue of the event. It comes from the lips of David and is directed toward Goliath. It is a dialogue filled with contrasts and faith.

David faces the uncircumcised Goliath, not just as the Israelites' representative, but as the Lord's representative! He stands not in his own name, Saul's name, or Israel's name, but in the name of the *Lord of Hosts*! He puts his life in the hands of God—and ONLY God. Like Daniel and the three Hebrew sons years later during the reign of Nebuchadnezzar, David publicly ties his own future to the will and providence of Almighty God, the universe's Commander-in-Chief (cf. Ps. 18:10-12).

David declares that Goliath has placed himself not in opposition to Saul or Israel, but in opposition to the Lord God Himself. He has dared to boast himself above the Lord of Hosts. Recalling Leviticus 24:16,

David notifies Goliath that he has committed a capital crime. *This* is why David chooses to pick up stones! He even mocks Goliath, throwing back into the giant's face his own terms of the "birds of the sky" and "beasts of the field" to describe his upcoming fate. It is Goliath vs. Yahweh. Who will prevail?

Then, it happens! With machine gun-like verbs, the battle erupts. The "champion" is struck (possibly hit in a chink of the armor near the knee) and falls forward on his face. The entire event is summarized briefly in verse 50. Goliath is down, but he is not out. The conflict is not over! A reminder is tagged to the summary—there is *no sword* in David's hand! David remains vulnerable to a counter-punch of lethal aggression.

David's adrenaline pumps. He runs, stands over the Philistine, takes the champion's own sword, draws it from its sheath, kills Goliath, and cuts off his head for all to see. The Philistines run like scalded dogs (pun from Goliath's words in verse 43 intended) and are chased by the armies of Israel for 10 miles.

WHO'S IN CHARGE?: THE BATTLE BELONGS TO THE LORD, NOT US

Notice Israel's response: they gather the spoils. Notice the king's response (vv. 57-58): he asks David, "Who are you?" Notice David's response sandwiched between those two parties: he brings gifts to God. He dedicates to God the most prized rewards of this conflict as reminders that the battle always belongs to the Lord (cf. 21:9, when he forgets).

God may have already anointed David as a leader, but he makes no attempt to use this event to manipulate his rise to power. He is absolutely *unimpressed* with himself, but he is marvelously and wonderfully impressed *with God!* The word spreads quickly that there is indeed a God in Israel who is mighty and to be feared, revered, worshipped, and served.

WHO'S IN CHARGE?: THE HISTORICAL PURPOSE AND THEOLOGICAL PURPOSE

Is this event about personal courage? Uncompromising determination? The armor of Goliath? The five stones of David? Human ingenuity?

Like most biblical narratives, the *historical purpose* is found at the end of the story. It introduces David as an unexpected emerging character in the life of the Israelites, juxtaposed to the comical King Saul. Like the exodus, the Red Sea, Mount Sinai, and the conquest of the Land of Promise, this event is cosmic in the life of God's people. Notice the amount of dialogue and character development focused on David. This marks the emergence of a true national deliverer and righteous leader under God's favor to restore the people of God to the Kingship of God.

However, like most biblical stories, the *theological purpose* is found near the middle. It answers the "who" and the "why" questions. It also answers the question, *"Who's in control here?"* Look at verses 45-46 again. Notice that in David's dialogue, Yahweh is the primary cause and focus. *He is the Who.* It is *His* battle, not David's. It is *His* work of grace, not David's athletic skill or military prowess. God does not depend on Saul's armor or David's skill or deliverance by any human means. It is never by our size, intelligence, techniques, status, titles, or social position, but only by His Spirit that we experience God—the battle is always His (v. 47; cf. Zech. 4:6).

The "why" is at the end of verse 46 and continues in verse 47. It is a purpose clause that includes an expression found *only three times* in the historical narrative after the exodus. The purpose is *global* in scope and *missionary* in nature: ". . .so that *all the earth*. . .*may know* that there *is* a God in Israel" (italics added).

Then look at verse 47 (NAS) ". . .and so that all *this assembly*. . .*may know* that the Lord does not deliver by sword or spear" (italics added). This is the third dimension, and it is local in its effect. It is directed toward the people of God themselves.

David hopes the whole world, beginning with the people of God themselves, will see that there is a God who is almighty, great, and holy (vv. 46-47; cf. Josh. 2:10-11).

This event is not so much about,

- David's courage but his loyalty;
- The aim of David's sling but the aim of his soul;
- The five stones but the one true God;
- The skill of the shepherd boy but the sovereignty of the Shepherd God;
- David's greatness but God's grace;
- The reputation of Israel but the reputation of God; and
- David being promoted in the nation but that the Lord will be worshipped throughout all the earth.

Does our world need to see that God is almighty, great, and holy? Do you need to experience Him in your own personal world?

This is the real purpose: *That the world may know that there is a God, that He can be known and trusted, and that He acts in history. He shows Himself on behalf of the weak, the overlooked, the runts, the least likely, and anyone whose heart of loyalty opens toward Him.* No earthly leader—local, national, or international —can compare!

So who's in charge here? Me? You? An unbelieving culture? Deacons? Elders? Denominational leaders? Who is king among God's people?

Your challenges today may be overwhelming. Your resources may be limited. The attacks may be psychological, and you may hear ridicule from others. But like David, you can take the weapon of faith, fashioned by God Himself, and watch God turn the tide.

Whatever faces you today, keep your heart focused on one great purpose—that all the earth may know our God. He commissions us for this purpose (Matt. 28:18-20). He empowers us for this purpose (Acts 1:8).

There is a real Leader among God's people. There is a true King in the Kingdom. This is the God by whom and to whom we are called. This is the God who deserves—yes, even commands—all our devotion and loyalty. It is our undeserved privilege to serve on His behalf.

What a God! What a King! Blessed is the people whose God is *this* Lord. May we be unimpressed with ourselves, but overwhelmingly impressed with Him! For when He is in control, all is under control. ᴄᐷᴏ

What Are You Out Of?
(John 2:1-11)

DR. MARVIN T. SMITH

Mt. Olive Institutional MBC
Saginaw, Michigan

Calvino Inman had just stepped out of the shower when a glimpse of his reflection in the mirror caused him to panic. You may not recognize him by name but perhaps by his rare condition: he's the boy who cries blood. When his mother, Tammy, saw his eyes streaming tears of blood, she immediately rushed him to the emergency room; but by the time they arrived, the bleeding had stopped.

They returned home, completely perplexed. A few days later, the bloody tears returned, so Calvino was rushed back to the hospital. Tammy hoped that maybe now the doctors would give them answers, but that wasn't the case. The doctors said that they'd never seen anything like it. After an MRI, a CT Scan, and an ultrasound, they still had no answers. Once again, though desperate for answers, Tammy and her son were sent home with the words, "We don't know how to stop it. It just has to run its course."

The jobless rate is the highest it has been in 26 years. Two hundred and sixteen thousand jobs were lost in August 2009 alone. Robert Gundee, the CEO of BackTrack, a national pre-employment background screening company, says the high unemployment rate makes some people so desperate for jobs that they will lie on resumés and job applications. Gundee went on to say that nearly 40% of resumés contain some type of lie during normal times, but it gets much worse when there are bad times. *Desperate people do desperate things!*

Take King Saul, the leader of God's people, who was so desperate about his future that he made an appointment with the witch of Endor. In Saul's desperation, he sought the very source that he had formerly removed from the land and risked his life by venturing into Philistine territory. At times, we do take desperate steps and make desperate cries, don't we?

The poet says:

> Desperate cries to the gods above;
> Desperate cries to the one I love;
> Desperate cries to cover the lives;
> Desperate cries to conceal the fear in my eyes!

Desperate moments can take you over the edge! We've seen people lose it when the doctors couldn't help, when the psychic's prediction was wrong, or when the horoscope reading was confusing. Are you out of something you desperately need? Is your life on "empty"? Have you run out of hope, joy, or peace? What or whom are you turning to for help? *You can turn to Jesus in times of desperation, and He can help you.*

Turn your attention for a moment to the wedding scene in John 2. The wedding takes place not far from Nazareth in the small village where the disciple Nathaniel lives: Cana of Galilee. A wedding in those days was a great celebration—no little 20-minute ceremony like ours. The ceremony usually took place late in the evening, on Wednesday; if the girl was a virgin, Thursday; if she was a widow, after the feast.

Then there was a procession, like a noisy parade, to the groom's house with entertainment that went on for at least a week. The guest list for this wedding included Jesus, His mother Mary and the disciples, and they all RSVP'ed. Even though Jesus was a man of sorrows and acquainted with grief, He was also a man who went to parties and enjoyed healthy conversation, laughter, and good food. (Some of us are so religious that we're rigid, but not Jesus.)

But in the midst of this joyous social affair came the possibility of great embarrassment: "They have no wine." This was a serious matter. There was a rabbinic adage that said, "Without wine there is no joy." They were not advising people to get drunk. Instead, this saying reflected the fact that in the first century there were not many beverages. They didn't have the plentiful choices that we have today: they didn't serve Coca-Cola® with ice, tea with lemon, or coffee with one Equal® and one cream. All they had was water or wine! It was a social *faux pas*—a violation of accepted social rules, a false step—to run out of wine. Lawsuits were brought forth under these circumstances. The bridegroom could be fined or called a cheapskate. This was a serious matter!

What is acceptable in one culture is considered unacceptable by another culture. For instance, in China, if a person takes the last item of food without first offering it to others, it is an insult to the host. In America, a guest is expected to eat all of the food given to them as a compliment to the quality of the cooking. So, we must not think that this particular situation of running out of wine was a minor incident without financial, social, and legal consequences.

JESUS IS RELIABLE

In this moment of desperation, Mary approached Jesus. She didn't ask explicitly for a miracle, but her words appeared to look for nothing less. She expected Jesus to do something without demanding what that something was. In your moment of desperation, your crisis, your being without, have you considered asking Jesus for help?

Dr. Tony Evans was once trapped on an elevator. The immediate reaction of all of the people was panic. They were trapped, stuck, and couldn't get out. Some people were crying, "Help! Help! Help!" but it wasn't working.

Other people were banging on the door: *Bam, bam, bam!* No one was hearing all that noise, but those folks didn't care. They kept right on bang-ing. Desperate people do desperate things. They were crying out.

There was one calm man on the elevator—Dr. Evans. He simply walked to the other side, pulled out a latch, picked up the telephone, and waited. A voice on the other end said, "Is there a problem?" He said, "We're trapped on the elevator between the 10th and 11th floor. Can we get some help?" They responded, "We'll be right there."

Everybody had forgotten about the phone. They were so focused on being trapped that they forgot there was a phone link to the security depart-ment. Merely because Dr. Evans picked up the phone, they were released from their desperate situation. All the human effort they put forth—bang-ing and yelling—wouldn't work, but picking up the phone and asking for help did. They had to seek help using the connection.

In a similar manner, you can turn to Jesus in your time of desperation. He's willing to help you, and He can help you in any situation. *He's reliable.*

Mary placed the problem before Him, and He responded with, "Dear woman, why are you getting Me involved in this matter?" Though speaking politely, Jesus was putting distance between them. He had to act according to God's timetable, so He said, "My hour is not here yet." That is, the culminating moment of the crucifixion was why Jesus came. The cross is not to be viewed simply as a sad accident on a hillside but a glorious occasion that has provided our redemption!

JESUS IS RESOURCEFUL

Clearly, Mary didn't take Jesus' words to her, "Dear lady or woman, why involve me in this?", as a sharp rebuke. Instead, she encouraged the servants to obey Jesus, who instructed them to fill the six water jars. Each jar could hold 20 gallons. When Jesus was telling them to fill the jars to the brim, it meant that there was no chance of placing anything else in them. There were plenty of people, so there was plenty of water—water to wash their hands and feet as they entered the celebration! By the time the servants obeyed Jesus, 120 gallons of wine were made.

How long does it take to make wine? After picking the grapes, you need to crush them. The time it takes to accomplish this will, of course, depend on how many grapes you have. The same goes for the rest of the process that would be done that day (i.e., mix in pectic enzyme and a dissolved Campden tablet). The fruit mixture is covered and left to stand for 24 hours.

Then you need to make and add the water/sugar/citrus juice mixture, and let it stand until it's room temperature. Then you add the mixture to a bucket and combine it with yeast and yeast nutrient. (Let's say this process takes four to five hours, for argument's sake.) Then it is left for six days. If the foam is foaming on top on the seventh day, it is strained. The strained mixture is then left to ferment for several months (anywhere between three to 12 months). So there you go: after picking the grapes, the winemaking process takes six to 12 months, plus seven days.

But for Jesus, all it takes is a word! *He is resourceful.* A lot of people want to help you in your time of need but can't. Jesus can! Some people can help but won't. Jesus will! Jesus has enough to help all of us without running out of anything! The apostle Paul reminds us, "My God shall supply all your need according to His riches in glory in Christ Jesus" (Phil. 4:19). He gives us what we need. There is more wine than needed.

The first response to the miracle is from the master of ceremonies. He says, "Every man serves the Chardonnay first, and then when their swagger becomes a stagger, he breaks out the Boone's Farm, the Mad Dog 20/20—the cheap stuff. But you have kept the good stuff until now."

If your life is in chaos, if you do not know what to do or where to go, *turn to Jesus because He is willing to help you. Jesus has enough resources to help you. Also, you can turn to Jesus because He can help you like no one else can!*

The quality of this wine was so superior that the emcee had to say something. He said, "I've never had anything like this before." The miracle did something for and in the disciples. It revealed the Lord's glory and gave them a stronger foundation for their faith.

Likewise, Jesus has helped us time and time again. But there is more to the miracle than the miracle: the miracle is a sign. What is a sign? A sign is something that points beyond itself to something greater. It's not enough to simply know Jesus has some power; we must also know Him as Lord and Savior. There is a difference between *knowing about* Him and *knowing* Him.

JESUS DESIRES RELATIONSHIP

Sports buffs know a lot about athletes whom they've not even met. They can cite statistics on touchdowns, home runs, and points scored. Gossips know a bunch about the latest scoop on people they don't even talk to—who divorced who and who's hanging out with whom. Pop-culture junkies read the tabloids even though the people they are so interested in could pass them on the street without a nod. In the same way, we can come to church for years and only know about God. *True knowledge of God requires a personal relationship.*

- We can get a healing but not know Jesus, the Healer!

- We can get a breakthrough but not know Jesus, the Deliverer!

- We can have peace of mind but not know Jesus, the Prince of Peace!

The theme of the Gospel of John is, "that you may believe that Jesus is the Christ, the Son of the living God, and that by believing you may have life in His name" (John 20:31). He came so that you might have life abundantly. In other words, Jesus will give you life and help you to live it to the fullest. Only Jesus can do that. The world's supply runs out and can't be regained, but the joy Jesus gives is ever new. The world offers the best first; then when you're hooked, it leaves you hanging. But Jesus only gives what's best until that one day when we enjoy the final blessings of the kingdom of heaven with the King.

Until then, *turn to and trust Jesus in times of desperation.* The hymn-writer encourages us to do this:

> Ask what you will of the Savior
> And it shall not be in vain
> Call when you need His assistance
> He will hear when you call His name.

God's Victorious Procession
(2 Corinthians 2:14-17)

DR. MAURICE WATSON

Beulahland Bible Church
Macon, Georgia

On March 7, 1965, 600 civil rights leaders headed east out of Selma, Alabama, on U. S. Route 80. They were headed to Montgomery to voice their demands for the right of African Americans to vote. They only got as far as the Edmund Pettus Bridge (some six blocks away), where state and local lawmen attacked them with billy clubs and tear gas and then drove them back to Selma. That infamous day is known as Bloody Sunday. To some it may have been a crushing defeat, but two weeks later on March 21st, after receiving a court injunction and federalized protection, hundreds of people marched across that bridge. By the time they reached the state capital on March 25, they were 25,000 strong. Less than five months later, President Lyndon B. Johnson signed the Voting Rights Act of 1965.

What seemed to have been a crushing defeat was really the seed out of which a glorious victory sprouted. Sometimes our victory or defeat is not determined by what happened at any one moment or given day in our lives, but our victory can be declared in the light of the ultimate outcome of life.

Apparently, this is what Paul means in this text, because he also refers to a march that seems to lead to defeat but instead really leads to victory. This was a different kind of march—not a civil rights march but a military march that the Corinthian citizens were well aware of. In the ancient Greco-Roman world, when the Roman Empire conquered a nation, the military forces marched in a triumphant procession to celebrate their victory. The purpose of this procession was to flaunt the power of the victorious nation. By celebrating this way, they reassured themselves and reiterated that the Roman emperor held absolute dominion over the world.

In the procession, people lined up and down the street, cheering on their triumphant army. The victorious general, bedecked in a purple robe, led the procession with captured and defeated prisoners chained in humiliation to his chariot. Priests also marched in the procession, swinging their incense containers and filling the air with the sweet smell of victory. Those chained and humiliated prisoners were paraded through the streets, and when the procession was over, they were put to death. However, some of them were spared as a sign of mercy on the part of the victorious general. This is the public spectacle to which Paul refers when he says, "Now thanks be to God, who always leads us in triumph in Christ" (v. 14 NKJV). The English Standard Version captures it better: "But thanks be to God, who in Christ, always leads us in triumphal procession."

In this little illustration, Paul applies the image of a victorious general to Jesus Christ. By doing so, he is suggesting that it was not the Roman emperor who had ultimate power, but Jesus Christ, the absolute ruler of the world. Paul sees himself and all believers as defeated prisoners of war who are chained to the chariot of Christ. However, we are not being led in humiliation to our death; instead, we are being led in victory by Christ into eternal life. Paul is trying to tell us that because we have been conquered and captured by Christ, we have victory instead of defeat. We have life instead of death.

This victory has to do with our standing in Jesus Christ. Because of who we are in Jesus Christ, we are assured of having the victory.

YOU ARE VICTORIOUS BECAUSE YOU FOLLOW THE SAVIOR

Christ is leading us; that means we are following Him. Following Christ has some positive implications. First of all, *you have victory, even when it looks like you're defeated.* Using an interesting paradox, Paul speaks of captured and defeated prisoners of war who are being paraded in a triumphal procession, chained to the chariot of the victorious general. He describes our victory by using imagery of our defeat.

But don't allow the paradoxical imagery to throw you off. Throughout this section, beginning in chapter 2, verse 14 and ending in chapter 7, verse 4, Paul—over and over again—uses paradoxes when describing our position of strength in the midst of weakness. In chapter 3, verse 5, the apostle says, "We are insufficient to serve God, but God has made us sufficient." In chapter 4, verse 7, he says, "We have a treasure in clay pots." In chapter 5, verse 1, he says, "We have a house that will last forever." In chapter 6, verse 10, Paul says, "We are sorrowful yet always rejoicing; as poor, yet making many rich; as having nothing, yet possessing all things."

In chapter 2, Paul uses another paradox to describe our victory by talking about our defeat. He says that even though we are like prisoners who have been chained to the chariot of Jesus Christ after being conquered by Him, He is not leading us to our death; He is leading us to our life.

The apostle had been concerned about the Corinthian church. He had written a letter to them earlier of rebuke and correction, so he was worried whether or not the Corinthian church had received his letter joyfully. In fact, in verse 13, he said he was so worried about it that he had no rest in his spirit because he hadn't heard from Titus regarding how they had accepted his letter. Now, Paul has obviously heard good news from Titus—that the people in Corinth had received his letter graciously. So he breaks out in a hymn of praise: "Now thanks be to God who always leads us in triumph in Christ." Now, when I first looked at that statement, I found it problematic: What did Paul mean about God always leading us in triumph and victory? Life doesn't always look victorious, does it? Sometimes it doesn't seem like we have the victory.

In fact, when you look at Paul's own life, you can make a case that Paul himself didn't always walk in victory. In Iconium, Paul was stoned and left for dead. In Philippi, he and Silas were thrown in jail. He went to Thessalonica, and the citizens ran him out of town. He went to Berea, and the same thing happened. In Athens, the Greeks mocked him and laughed at him on Mars Hill. Then, he went to Ephesus and a riot broke out. He went to Jerusalem, and they arrested him in the temple. He went to Rome, and they killed him. So, life didn't always look victorious for Paul.

But the apostle is telling you that your victory is not defined by what happened in your life on any given day; your victory is determined by the outcome of your life. If you don't believe me, look at the example of Jesus. On Friday, He didn't look very victorious. On Friday, they put a cross on His shoulder. On Friday, they marched Him from judgment hall to judgment hall. On Friday, they put nails in His hands and His feet. They hung Him high, stretched Him wide, and dropped Him low. But all that time, Jesus was essentially saying, "Don't judge Me by the way things look on Friday because that's just the beginning of the weekend. If you're going to judge My victory, you've got to judge it by the whole weekend because I died on Friday but got up on Sunday."

That's why I can tell the person who got a pink slip on his desk at his job, "You can go on and praise God because that pink slip doesn't define who you are." That's why I can tell that person with cancer, "Whether you or live or die, He's leading you to victory." That's why I can tell that person with the wayward child, "God is leading you to victory because your victory is not determined by any one moment in your life." When you follow Christ, you have victory even when it doesn't look like it.

You also have victory because whatever you go through, He's already been through it; and He won. Paul said that we are like prisoners chained to Christ's chariot. That means He's leading us, which implies that whatever we go through, He's already been through it and has won the victory. Temptation? He faced that. Hebrews 4:15 says, "He was in all points tempted as we are, yet without sin." Storms? He went through that. In Mark 4:39, Jesus told the storm on the sea, "Peace, be still." What about rejection? He went through that. John 1:11 says, "He came to His own, and His own received Him not." Family problems? He went through that. His brothers and sisters didn't believe in Him at first. Financial problems? He went through that. In Luke 9:58, Jesus said, "Foxes have holes, birds have nests, but the Son of Man has nowhere to lay His head." Scandal? He went through that. His birth by a virgin was held in suspicion by the local townfolk. Depression? He went through that. He was depressed in the Garden of Gethsemane. In Matthew 26:38, Jesus said, "My soul is exceedingly sorrowful, even unto death." Are friends a disappointment to you? He went through that. Peter denied him three times. Do you have false friends? He went through that. Judas betrayed him. How about fair-weather friends? He went through that. They all forsook Him. Facing death? He went through that. He died on Friday. Have you experienced your lowest point in life? He went through that. He went to hell on Saturday. What about triumph? He went through that. He got up on Sunday.

You have victory because whatever you go through, He's already been through it and won. In conclusion, you are victorious because you follow the Savior.

YOU ARE VICTORIOUS BECAUSE OF THE FRAGRANCE YOU SPREAD

The apostle says, "Thanks be to God who always leads us in triumph in Christ and through us diffuses [that word "diffuses" means to manifest or spread] the fragrance of His knowledge in every place." Now Paul shifts metaphors and talks about fragrance—that God uses us to spread the aroma of His knowledge everywhere. Paul is saying that wherever the gospel is preached, we are spreading the fragrance, or the scent, of the Lord Jesus Christ. It's interesting that Paul uses this olfactory metaphor because a fragrance goes wherever it wants to go. In other words, it can't be contained. In fact, a fragrance can be so strong that it can be on another side of the door and you can still smell it.

New Testament scholar Mitzi Minor says that one can shut the doors and windows, douse the lights, refuse to eat or drink, and stick one's hands in one's pockets, thus shutting out the senses of sight, sound, taste, and touch; but a fragrance will seep in anyway—under and around doors and windows. In the same way, God uses us to diffuse the fragrance of the knowledge of the Lord Jesus Christ everywhere we go.

Now look at the irony of this: Paul speaks of this triumphal procession that the Roman Empire would stage to flaunt their absolute power over the world. Nevertheless, the same Roman Empire that tried to stop the church collapsed centuries ago, but the church is still in business. The church is still alive because you cannot contain the fragrance of the gospel of Jesus Christ.

Moreover, the aroma that we spread around us creates a crisis moment for others. Look at what Paul says in verses 15 and 16: "For we are to God the fragrance of Christ among those who are being saved and among those who are perishing. To the one we are the aroma of death, leading to death, and to the other we are the aroma of life, leading to life." Paul now pushes that metaphor even further. He says that not only does God use us to spread the fragrance of the message of Jesus Christ to the world, but we *are* that fragrance of Christ.

In that triumphal Roman procession, the priests lined the streets, swinging incense. All those prisoners chained to the chariot of the conquering general could smell the aroma from the incense as they were paraded down the streets. To those prisoners heading to the city square to be executed, that aroma was the aroma of death. But there were other prisoners who were spared; so for them, that aroma was not an aroma of death but of life.

Paul used the metaphor of a fragrance to emphasize that wherever the gospel is preached, a crisis moment is created, and the hearers cannot remain neutral. They have to make a decision—either to accept it and have life or reject it and have death. The apostle is saying to us that the gospel we preach has an aroma surrounding it. For those who accept the gospel, it is the sweet aroma of life; but for those who reject the gospel, it smells like a million dead corpses.

How does it smell when you hear the gospel? Does it make you want to say, "I don't want that, I don't believe that, or I'm not ready for that"? In that case, it's an aroma of death for you. On the other hand, are you like those who think the gospel smells good? If you want to embrace it because you realize how much you want Christ in your life, then the gospel is the aroma of life for you.

Let me ask a more personal question: How do you smell at work? How do you smell at home? How do you smell at school? Are you emitting the fragrance of Christ? Can people smell Christ on you? How do you smell when you're not at church?

YOU ARE VICTORIOUS BECAUSE YOU HAVE BEEN MADE FIT TO SERVE HIM

In light of the ramifications of what he has just said, Paul asks a question at the end of verse 16: "Who is sufficient for these things?" That word "sufficient" means competent or equal to the task. In other words, Paul, after identifying the life-and-death ramifications of the gospel, asks, "Who is sufficient in and of himself to handle such a word?" It is a rhetorical question. The obvious answer is, "No one is sufficient in and of himself." But Paul answers his own question in chapter 3, verses 5 and 6: "Not that we are sufficient of ourselves to think of anything as being from ourselves, but our sufficiency is from God, who also made us sufficient as ministers of the new covenant."

In other words, the only reason that God uses any one of us is because He has made us sufficient. God has made us fit to serve Him, because none of us deserve to be used by Him. All of us have faults and flaws and failures. I am not worthy to preach because I have let God down, but the fact of the matter is that God has made up for my shortcomings. Everyone God used in the Bible had some kind of shortcoming. Moses told God he couldn't speak well. Jeremiah informed God he was too young. Sarah claimed she was too old. Paul had a thorn in his flesh. Timothy had stomach problems. But God doesn't allow your shortcomings to stop Him from using you for His glory because He made you fit to serve Him.

YOU ARE VICTORIOUS BECAUSE YOU HAVE
BEEN FAITHFUL TO THE SCRIPTURES

Look at verse 17: "For we are not, as so many, 'peddling' the Word of God." Paul asks in verse 16, "Who is sufficient for these things?" He begins verse 17 with the connective word, "for," which implies that there were those in Paul's day who thought they were competent to handle the Word of God in themselves. That word "peddling" is a commercial word. It conveys the idea of a shabby businessman who sells wine, but he waters the wine down in order to stretch it; in short, he dilutes the wine. A "peddler" is someone who makes a profit selling shoddy goods. Paul is basically saying, "We are not, as so many, hucksters, peddlers, diluters of the Word of God."

Paul says that he is instead preaching the Word of God "but as of sincerity." (That is, his motives are pure.) The apostle continues, ". . .we speak in the sight of God in Christ." In other words, when we preach the gospel, we are not those who sent ourselves; instead, we have been commissioned or sent by God. When we preach, we preach out of our relationship with Christ—as if God were sitting in the audience. We need to be members of a church where the Word of God is preached and taught faithfully. When the Scriptures are taught with integrity, it leads us not to defeat, but it always leads us to victory.

Paul uses the imagery of us being in the triumphant procession. He says that we've been chained to the chariot of Jesus. "But, Jesus," we ask, "where are You leading us? What is going to happen at the end of this procession? Where are You trying to take us?" We can rest assured that He is not leading us to damnation, humiliation, failure, or a hopeless future; instead, He is leading us into victorious triumph. ⬧

The Church Goes On
(Matthew 16:18; 1 Timothy 3:15; 1 Corinthians 3:9)

PASTOR RALPH DOUGLAS WEST SR.

The Church Without Walls
Houston, Texas

There are some things that we used to think were everlasting. Architecturally, institutions that we once held high confidence in have fallen into that category, especially those in New York City. Financially, previously solid rocks of Gibraltar such as Merrill Lynch, Fanny Mae, Freddy Mac, AIG, and Bernstein can all be classified in the same way. Globally, investors are panicked by such drastic changes. Geographically, no one could have imagined that the Gulf Coast communities in New Orleans, Mississippi, Alabama, and Texas could have been as devastated by clashing waves and high winds the way they were. Besides all these world-changing news items, subprime mortgage rates have affected each of us in one way or another. Things that we once thought were impenetrable have now dissipated into nothing.

The well-known African American folklore writer, Mark Cantly, who wrote about green pastures, paints a scene of the angel Gabriel in upper Manhattan, New York, peering out of his apartment and observing the human traffic passing by. While doing so, he reports in an old dialect, "Today Lawd, eva thang a nailed down is a comin' loose." We feel like this in so many ways. We have always believed everything was fixed and fitted together, but those very permanent fixtures seem to be coming loose.

People often ask if there is anything viable, durable, visible, and unchangeable that we can latch onto that will provide us sure footing. The answer is clearly "yes." *We can put our confidence in—and stand upon the certainty of—the hope that the church of the Lord Jesus Christ goes on.*

There are three images directly associated with the church in New Testament literature. Even though hundreds can be used, these three are directly associated with the *ecclesia*, "the called-out ones."

The first image is found in Matthew 16:18. In this passage, Jesus is in a "question-and-answer" session with His disciples. Public opinion has already circulated throughout the community. In Caesarea Philippi, Jesus asks His disciples, "What is the popular opinion poll registering about My identity?" Simon Peter says, "Some say that You are one of the prophets," and he names a few of those prophets. Jesus then moves from the general to the specific by asking, "Well, who do you say that I am?" Peter blurts out his confession, "Thou art the Christ, the Son of the Living God." In that regard, when we make that faith confession, all of us stand in the sandals of Simon Peter. In the words of Martin Luther, "We are all Peters at that point" as we make confessions of faith that "Thou art the Christ."

According to Paul in Ephesians 2:20, the layer of the foundation of the church has been laid: "The foundation is laid first by the prophet and then by the apostles." First Peter 2:5 says, "[We] also, [are] like living stones…to God through Jesus Christ." The church is not a dead, still, static place. The church is the living, viable presence of the living Lord on planet Earth.

THE CHURCH GOES ON BECAUSE THE GATES OF HELL SHALL NOT OVERTHROW IT

In Matthew 16:18, Jesus indicates that His relationship to the church is one of *construction*. Jesus says, "I will build My church." In essence Christ is saying, "I will be the architect and construct My church. I am the builder and the designer, so I will supply the material. What I build, only I can build. I will build My church."

He goes on to make another statement relating to construction—that is, of *possession*: "My church." That is, He is the owner of the church. Regarding the church and *confrontation*, He says, "[A]nd the gates of Hell shall not prevail against it."

What is verse 18 actually saying, as it relates to you and the church going on? In every sense, this statement suggests that no formidable foe can stand against the church. That is, tsunamis, fires, hurricanes, tornadoes, or death itself cannot stand against it. Regardless of what power each of these disasters may have, all of them will fail in comparison to the power of the living Lord Jesus Christ. Nothing will be able to stop the church because the church goes on! This is somewhat of a "Duracell theology": we can take a licking but keep on ticking. For you as a believer, it becomes evident that as the church goes on, you also can go on.

There are many churches that are noted for their durability. One such church, located in East Houston, is the First Baptist Church of Pasadena, which was leveled many years ago by a tornado. Those congregants still gathered together outside on the parking lot and had church. Some of the members believe that they had better church services outside on the parking lot than they did all of the years they were inside the church. One reason for this is that when all of their security trappings had been taken away from them, the only person whom they could depend on and rely upon was God Himself. Every once in a while, the Lord will pull the security blanket from beneath us to remind us that He alone has been sustaining us. Thus, buildings, businesses, entrepreneurs, and investments can disappear; but the church goes on.

God has unusual, strange, peculiar, queer ways of getting us in places where He wants us to be. In the biographical material on Helmut

Thielicke, you will discover some interesting things. Thielicke pastored the Cathedral Church in Germany during World War Two. In his autobiography *Notes from a Wayfarer* he says, "I pastored during a time when modern topics and clichés would not attract people to church. Well, my congregation found themselves in severe loss of property, material, and family. There they waited on a word that would come from God."

Thielicke wrote from experience because he actually took part in the suffering. His home was burned down. The church where he pastored was torched; in fact, the only thing that he had left was the key to the door that no longer existed. When that church burned to ashes, not even a frame or perhaps just a side wall was left. The area where 3,000 people gathered was all gone, but they did not run away or question their next move. They did not look at the rubble with downcast faces, saying that it was all over now. They did not say that the last bastion of hope had been taken away from them. Every member of that church in that war-torn community and city got up and walked to the church. They stood there among its ashes to hear a word from God. Apologizing for his dress, Pastor Thielicke stood there in his war boots and preached the hope and faith that comes from trusting the Lord Jesus Christ. He reminded them that the building may be blown up and burned down, but the church goes on.

God alone has the power to restore your life to a place beyond your imagination. God alone has the way of bringing all things together. Your presence is evidence of that. You are a faithful member of the church regardless of your situation and circumstances, which indicates in and of itself that the church is going on.

THE CHURCH GOES ON BECAUSE THE CHURCH IS THE PILLAR AND FOUNDATION OF TRUTH

First Timothy is a letter Paul wrote to his young apprentice Timothy for him to read to the church of Ephesus. When he reached the third chapter of the letter in verse 15, Paul said, "Timothy, I am writing this so that you will know how to conduct yourselves in the house of God, the pillar and the foundation of truth." As Timothy read this, the image that probably came to his mind was sparked by the words "*pillar*" and "*foundation*." As a resident of Ephesus, he was aware of the 127 Ionic columns in the temple of Diana. His mind immediately recalled those columns, and he knew that they were displaying the splendor of the temple. When he read the word "foundation," he understood that it was the bulwark—the impenetrable, impregnable, durable foundation. Paul said, "This is how you are to behave in the household of God, the pillar and the foundation of truth," which simply led into the very next words: "This is what these pillars look like."

The pillars were symbolic of viability and durability; that is, they had a lasting presence. In this portion of the letter, Paul had given to Timothy what he was to hold up. He says in couplets with a musical tone, "In the church, hold up these things: the manifestation of Christ in the flesh and the vindication of Christ in the spirit, the angelic observation and the universal proclamation, the reception of Christ in the Earth and also the glorification of Christ in the Heavens" (v. 16). That was Paul's way of saying, "Preach the Kerygma: preach that Christ was born, walked among us, died on a cross, was buried, and rose on Easter morning. He ascended into heaven 50 days later, is now seated at the right hand of the Father, and left the Holy Spirit with us."

Regardless of what pressure your life might be under, you are never alone because the church goes on. In Ephesus, the pillars that have fallen down can be named. The pillars of Hadrian and Artemis are no more; they are all gone. In fact, the only pillars that still stand are the pillars of truth. We serve a living Savior who died, was buried, arose, and is here right now. These are the pillars of truth, and they rest on the foundation. The truth does not rest on the church; instead, the church rests on the truth.

Samuel J. Stone might not be a familiar name in the church of today, but his musical stanzas are. In 1866, at the height of critical interpretation of the Scripture, prominent and influential bishops of the Anglican church wrote a trilogy of books. They refuted the authenticity of the first five books of the Old Testament and Joshua: the Hexateuch. (It is one thing for the gates of hell to attack from the outside, but it is quite another thing when the pillars of truth are being attacked from within.)

This divisive, internal, brewing controversy was causing a schism within the church. Stone began reading through the Apostles' Creed, and from that statement of faith he wrote a hymn called, "The Church's One Foundation." One of those stanzas simply said, "The church's one foundation is Jesus Christ the Lord/She is the new creation, born by water and the Word/From Heaven He sought her to be His holy bride/With His own blood He bought her and for her life He died." The one foundation of the church is Jesus Christ our Lord; that is our hope.

People say many things pertaining to the church. They make fun of and even laugh at the church. They degrade the church and call preachers hypocritical and inauthentic. An amazing fact is that when real trouble comes, no one scorns the church at that point.

The church helps strangers and prays for them; the church is always there. Jesus is happy with the church. If He had to explain His happiness, He would say, "When I was hungry, you fed Me. When I was thirsty, you gave Me water. When I had no clothes, you clothed Me. When I was marginalized and destitute, you came by to check on Me."

Some of you might have come from a background that gave you a low estimation of the church. That is, church did not mean much to you; it was simply a place to go and do something. I am fortunate to have been reared in a church that was truly a church. You should want that for yourself. You should want to be in a church where the pillar and the foundation is the Lord Jesus Christ.

THE CHURCH GOES ON BECAUSE YOU ARE GOD'S BUILDING

In 1 Corinthians 3, Paul is responding to the divisive human leadership issue that has become a controversy in the church. The apostle uses three images in verse 9: *you are God's coworkers, you are God's field, and you are God's building*. Prior to that, Paul discusses the particular issue regarding some people within the Corinthian congregation who linked their conversions with specific persons. Some said, "My conversion is a result of the baptism of John." Others said, "My conversion is a result of Simon Peter." Still others claimed, "My conversion is a result of Apollos." Then, some others insisted, "Mine is a result of Paul." Paul disagreed with all of them, saying that we instead are *coworkers* with God.

Then Paul continued, "We are God's field." The Husbandman has cultivated all of our lives; that is where fruitfulness comes. One plants, another waters, and then God gives the increase.

Then Paul comes back and says, "You are God's building." Any name can be inserted here; the emphasis falls on "*you*." A mere reading of this verse will change something in you. One reason for this is simply the idea that God would trust His future in you: you are God's building.

A trip to Corinth today would reveal some fascinating truths that are worth noting. The first observation is that thousands of tourists visit there. Without burdening you with a heavy archaic speech about antiquity, let's take a journey across the waters to this land. Pay attention to what is there, but give more of your attention to what is not there. As you walk down modern-day Corinth on the isthmus, the Adriatic and the Aegean Seas are still there. But as you walk through ancient Corinth and remember those buildings that were built with gold, silver, and precious stones, you will notice that they are all gone—all of the temples, columns, and pillars. Yet, every single day thousands of tourists come to that piece of isthmus by yacht, boat, plane, or bus and walk in Corinth to look at what is no longer there.

The question might arise, "If the buildings are no longer there, what brings these people here? Why would anyone want to see what they can no longer see?" The answer to those questions is simple. People go to the ruins of Corinth because a man named Paul lived there, and a little church of approximately 250 members was established there. Even though the apostle and the house church in Corinth are gone, the letter to the Corinthians is still in our hands. People read this letter and make a conscious decision to go and see one of the places that helped exponentially spread Christianity throughout the world. In reality, the towers, temples, and buildings may be gone; but Christ is still there. The sheer evidence of this is the Bible, and that means the church goes on!

If there was ever a church that should have gone out of business, it should have been the one in Corinth. It doesn't take a critical reader of the New Testament to understand this. Any good English translation of the Bible will reveal that the Corinthian church should have gone out of business. The first four chapters involve controversies of human leadership. Chapter 5 discusses the controversy of immorality within that particular church fellowship. Chapter 6 deals with the controversy over legal matters regarding who can go to court and who cannot. Chapter 7 addresses the controversy over marriage. Chapters 8, 9, and 10 focus on controversies over dietary, customary, and ritual/religious laws. Chapter 11 speaks to the controversy over the Lord's Supper. Chapters 12, 13, and 14 concentrate on controversies over the spiritual gifts. Chapter 15 tackles the controversy regarding the historical resurrection of Jesus Christ. Chapter 16 attends to a controversy over tithing. Notice that each controversy is enough to completely destroy modern-day churches.

No person would presume to discipline and develop a church without reading about the early Corinthian congregation. First Corinthians proves to us that the church of the Lord Jesus is not built by human imagination but by the Spirit, the water, and the blood of Christ—that is, by one Lord, one faith, and one baptism. If it were not for the foundation of the Lord Jesus Christ, the church would have already gone out of business. Since Christ is the foundation, however, nothing can stop the church.

Everything else might be falling, but the church is still going. In fact, in the face of trouble the church blossoms the most. Remember that the church did not get started when you were converted; the church has been here for a long time. From its inception, people have tried to stop the church. From ancient to modern times, there have been movements afoot to derail the church, but they have never succeeded.

In A. D. 70, for example, Nero attempted to stop the church by setting Rome on fire and blaming the Christians for it. Domitian carried out the same traitorous works as his successor, persecuting various believers. Then Decius took over and decided to re-establish emperor worship; those that did not comply experienced different kinds of oppression and persecution. His successor, Valerian, began to slay Christians.

After them, the bloodthirsty Diocletian became emperor. Anyone who studies church history knows his name because of the blood stain that his reign left; Diocletian was killing believers everywhere. He put the bishops in prison and then the presbyters. Next, he put the clerics in prison and declared that he would wipe the streets with their blood. When Diocletian retired, he had to find a successor; but instead of choosing just one successor, he appointed two co-emperors: Maximianus and Constantine. In an unsuccessful attempt to coexist, a fight occurred and Constantine won. His son, who inherited his name, had a vision of the cross and was converted and baptized. The Roman Empire, which was trying to kill the people, became a patrimonial! That is, the Pax Romana (peace of Rome) provided all kinds of access to Christians, so Christianity kept going. When Diocletian appointed Constantine as co-emperor, he had no idea what God had in mind for his replacement. Likewise, God can—and just might—use your enemies to become your footstool!

In World War Two, St. Isaac's Cathedral on St. Isaac's Square in St. Petersburg, Russia, was the largest church in Russia. It took 40 years to build that church. During the war, the church was closed down when the Communists threw the Christians out. Moreover, they turned St. Isaac's Church into a theatre of atheism. They replaced the dove at the top of the dome with a Foucault pendulum to signify their belief that science was really what made the world move. Atop the dome had been a mosaic of the Lord Jesus Christ looking down on the people as they came in to worship, but it was painted gray to avoid attention from passing enemy aircraft. Throughout those war-torn years, the temple that was once a church was converted into a museum, and the shrine of atheism became a potato farm. (People dragged dirt into the church and planted potatoes during the war.) With the fall of Communism, the museum closed and the church re-opened. The church re-opened, but it was never really closed down. In the darkest, gloomiest days, the church goes on. ◌◌

Overcoming the Spirit of the Crowd
(Luke 19:1-10)

BISHOP KENNETH WHITE

Linconia Tabernacle Christian Center
United Holy Church of America
Trevose, Pennsylvania

SMALL BEGINNINGS

In July of 1963 a child was born to a poor couple by the name of Webb. They decided to name their son Anthony Jerome. While raising Anthony in a small home in the city of Dallas, Texas, the Webb family soon realized that their baby boy's development was not like that of other children. He was not growing at the same pace as other children his age. As a matter of fact, it became more and more obvious that little Anthony would probably remain "Little" Anthony, and his short stature would always be something that he would have to contend with in one way or another.

As Anthony grew, sports became his outlet; however, he was often times overlooked by his school's athletics teams or chosen only when there was no one else to pick. Eventually Anthony began to excel at the game of basketball. He used his quickness and jumping ability to outplay the other kids. No one could touch him when it came to his running ability, and no one could outjump him either! He found out that, even though he was short in stature, he had a God-given ability to jump very high. At five-foot-five inches tall, he tried out for his high school basketball team and was told that he could only play on the junior varsity team. But Anthony did so well that he was soon placed on the varsity team and later recruited by a junior college. Soon afterward, Webb attracted the attention of the coaching staff at North Carolina State University, where he received a basketball scholarship. While attending there, his teammates gave him the nickname "Spud." In 1985, Spud Webb was drafted in the fourth round of the NBA draft by the Detroit Pistons, and a year later he made history by becoming the shortest person to ever win the NBA's renowned slam-dunk contest.

This is quite an amazing story, but this scenario is not all that unheard of! Just like Spud Webb, many of us have had to grow up with an impediment or some kind of disadvantage that caused people to look upon us as if we were incapable or somehow lesser than others. Spud Webb's story was one that I could relate to so well because it reminded me of my own childhood. I was born with a speech impediment that caused me to stutter more than what was considered normal. Speech therapy was probably not as widely available back then as it is today, but I am sure that it was not even considered by my parents. My father stuttered, his brother stuttered, and there were some on my mother's side of the family who stuttered as well. I was laughed at so much in school that I would get into fight after fight in reaction to the way the kids made fun of my stammering tongue. The discipline I received because I did not want to read aloud in class or in Sunday school became a regular occurrence. I even remember going to the altar and telling an evangelist that I wanted God to heal me of stuttering. She prayed for me and then told me to drink eight glasses of water a day for two weeks to help me with my stuttering problem. Like Spud Webb and many of you, I too had to learn how to make the best of a situation that was not going to change. My speech impediment followed me from high school into college. The teasing did not stop, but I learned how to handle it without being aggressive. My parents taught me to pray before I spoke! Little did I know that this was in line with Philippians 4:13, which says, "I can do all things through Christ who strengthens me."

Just for a moment, I want you to think about how much we all have in common with one another—even with the Webb family! I know that you may not want to think about it because you would much rather put that chapter of your life behind you, but there are benefits to remembering from whence you have come. There is a Scripture that says, "For who hath despised the day of small things?" (Zech. 4:10). Reflecting upon your small beginnings or the things of your past that you thought you would never overcome will help you to better appreciate all of the wonderful things that God is doing in your life now. I'm sure that Mr. Webb had dreams for his family, but it didn't seem as if they would take place in his lifetime. The Webb family's story, your story, and my story all testify to the awesome power of God! In fact, Mark 10:27 says, *"For with God all things are possible!"*

"SHORT" COMINGS!

Every word in the Scriptures has its significance. As I considered the 19th chapter of Luke's gospel, several things came to mind. First, I wanted to know what brought Jesus to Jericho. Was it business or was Jesus just en route to another place that He was scheduled to appear? I was then reminded of a verse in the fourth chapter of John, when the writer said that "Jesus needed to go through Samaria." Thus, I concluded that just as Jesus' assignment took him through Samaria to help a young woman, this assignment recorded in Luke's gospel also demanded that Jesus go to a town to set someone free. Prior to Jesus' entering the town of Jericho, He comes in contact with a certain blind man who was begging. The Scripture does not give this man a name; he's simply given the label of a beggar.

(Have you ever been labeled? Labels can haunt you! Labels can also cause you to miss your season if you are not carefully focused. What if

Spud Webb succumbed to being labeled too short to play basketball? Think about that while we further explore the Scriptures.)

The Bible doesn't say what this blind man was begging for. It is interesting to note that this is the same blind man referred to in Mark 10—Bartimaeus. Even though Luke did not deem it important enough to give him a name, Jesus considered this man important enough to come to Jericho. The Bible says that the beggar sensed the gathering of the crowd, and he inquired about what was causing such a commotion. Somebody in the crowd told him that Jesus was passing through the city. The beggar sensed that this was his perfect opportunity to receive healing and deliverance, so he began to holler uncontrollably, "JESUS, SON OF DAVID!" He was told to be quiet, but he sensed that his deliverance was within reach. The voices that were trying to stop him could not stop the fact that he had made up his mind that deliverance belonged to him!

Please note that the first step to your healing and deliverance is a made-up mind. When you come to the place of worship, you have to make up your mind and say to yourself, *"This is my day for deliverance!!! This is my day for healing!!! This is my day for answered prayer!!! This is my day for promises to be fulfilled, and I will let nothing stop me from getting it!!!"*

This man was so set on what he needed from the Lord that he knew if he could just get Jesus' attention, it would put him right in line for his miracle. I believe there was something in his voice that touched the heart of Jesus!!! Perhaps there was possibly something about his cry that Jesus could not ignore. Jesus asked the man, "What do you want Me to do for you?" The man responded, "That I might receive my sight." Jesus answered, "Receive your sight, your faith has made you well" (Luke 18:41-42 NKJV). Immediately the man regained his sight and followed Jesus, glorifying God.

Luke wanted us to know that this miracle took place in or near a well-populated place: Jericho. This city was known for its crowds as well as its ability to produce. Known as the "City of Palm Trees," Jericho was also recognized for its main commodity—olive oil. Oil has always represented *the anointing or the Spirit* in the Scriptures. Luke also wanted us to know that the presence of God was there to perform miracles. Likewise, just as the beggar sensed the presence of Jesus through what he was hearing (in spite of the crowds), so can we! Romans 10:17 (KJV) says, "… faith cometh by hearing; and hearing by the word of God."

Jesus uses this story of healing blind Bartimaeus in chapter 18 to preface the marvelous deliverance of Zacchaeus in chapter 19. At first glance I did not see the correlation between the two chapters; but as I continued to read the story, the Lord put it in my spirit that Zacchaeus must have overheard Jesus talking and perhaps heard of the beggar's miracle. Let's explore how these two passages of Scripture connect. Both men had something that was stopping them from seeing Jesus. Zacchaeus heard Jesus but could not see Him because he was too short, while the beggar (blind Bartimaeus) heard Jesus but could not see Him because he was blind. Ask yourself this question: "What is stopping me from seeing. . .Jesus?"

Zacchaeus was a rich tax collector. History shows us that this job might have been considered the job of a lifetime in that day. It was a high-paying job that put Zacchaeus in what would be considered a higher tax bracket in comparison to today's standards, but his job obviously didn't fulfill all of his desires. Namely, his job could not add one inch to his stature. He was rich, but he still had to deal with the ridicule and laughter of others for being short. He had a well-paying job, but he still had desires that weren't being met! He was rich but unsatisfied! Verse 3 says, ". . .he sought to see Jesus." (I wish for the day when the saints of God would whole-heartedly "*seek after Jesus!*")

In the 11th chapter of Luke, Jesus gave instructions to His disciples concerning prayer. In verses 9 and 10 (NKJV) He said, "So I say to you, ask, and it will be given to you; seek, and you will find; knock, and it will be opened. For everyone who asks receives, and he who seeks finds, and to him who knocks it will be opened." There are rewards for those who will seek after Jesus! Seeking suggests consistency—not an "every-now-and-then" worship—but rather a consistency in worship! I submit to you that he who asks will receive, he who seeks will find, and unto him who knocks, it will be opened!

Zacchaeus found out that it pays to seek Jesus. He sought Jesus in spite of what was going on in his personal life. He had a desire to find Him even though he encountered a hindrance: there was a crowd that was in his way. This Scripture passage does not say how many people made up the crowd; it just says, "because of the crowd. . ." I have come to realize that in some folks' lives, it does not take much to hinder or stop them. To some, a crowd can be one person. To others, a crowd could be many things! Sometimes there are even thoughts that can crowd one's mind. I like the fact that the Bible does not define Zacchaeus' crowd.

Whatever or whoever the crowd was, it caused Zacchaeus to want to go higher. The Bible says he climbed in order to get above his crowd. Can you imagine a child trying to see something so bad that he or she runs around, looking for any opening to peer through? There's an intense desire to see, yet there's a crowd standing in the way. Zacchaeus' crowd may have been his short stature. People probably teased him during childhood and perhaps even as an adult. His short height was his crowd!

Are you able to identify the crowd in your life? Can you see Jesus clearly from the position that you are in? Do you desire to go higher in order to get above your crowd?

When Zacchaeus decided to climb up above his hindrance, then Jesus saw him! Verse 5 says, "And when Jesus came to the place. . ." What place? I believe it was the place where Zacchaeus climbed. The Scripture says that it was a sycamore tree, but it really doesn't matter what kind of tree it was. What matters is that Jesus stopped at the place where Zacchaeus climbed. Jesus stopped right at the place where Zacchaeus made a decision to get above his crowd.

Any of you who have ever had to face a crowd in your life can relate to the story of Zacchaeus. If you have been beat down so much because of an impediment or disadvantage, then that represents the crowd in your life. Yet when Jesus saw that Zacchaeus was willing to ignore the crowd and put himself in a position to be blessed in the face of his short-comings, that is when He acknowledged Zacchaeus and invited Himself to his house.

JESUS WANTS TO COME TO YOUR HOUSE

Have you pinpointed the crowd in your life yet—or perhaps the crowd in your mind? Does it seem like every time something good is about to come out of your situation, along comes negative people? They may be considered a crowd as well! I'm sure that there were people there who didn't want Zacchaeus to overcome his situation. They were happy that Jesus was coming to his house, but probably happier that he had let the crowd block his blessing for so long. The Message Bible records the crowd's comments in this way: "What business does Jesus have getting cozy with that crook Zacchaeus...?" In other words, they tried to block his deliverance!

There are times when the things that block you will also be the same things that will cause you to go higher. It is in these times that we must be thankful for the crowd. It was because of the crowd that Zacchaeus was able to say, "Jesus, I'll give half of my income to the poor... and if I've cheated anyone, I'll pay it back four times over..." When you really overcome the spirit of the crowd, even your thinking changes! When you really get delivered from the crowd, you'll get happy when you hear Jesus say; *"Today salvation has come to your house!"*

There is another person in the Scriptures who was hindered by the crowd, as recorded in the 5th chapter of John's gospel. The Bible says that in Jerusalem there was a pool called Bethesda that was surrounded by five porches, located near the Sheep Gate. Those who had sicknesses and ailments came and gathered there. Once a year the Angel of the Lord came down and stirred the water of this pool. The story says that whoever got in first would be made whole. Unfortunately, there was a man who had been waiting to get into this pool for 38 years but couldn't because of the hindrance of the crowd. The Bible describes this crowd as a *"great multitude of impotent folk"* (v. 3 KJV).

On this particular occasion, Jesus came and asked the man if he wanted to be made whole, and he openly admits to being hindered by the crowd. I implore you *not to allow a great multitude of impotent folk to hinder you from getting your deliverance from Jesus!* In other words, don't let weak, ineffective, and powerless people stop you from seeing Jesus! You will know who these people are by how they try to make your impediment appear normal. They will ask you things such as, "Why are you going to church so much?" They may even be in the church asking things such as, "Why do you keep going to the altar every Sunday?"

Jesus wants to come into your house just as he did with Zacchaeus! He wants to see you made whole just like the man at the pool of Bethesda! But seeing Jesus will always hinge upon a decision. In both cases, these men decided that it was their day to receive all of the blessings that Jesus had in store for their lives. Ultimately, you too can receive all that Jesus has for you by opening up your heart and allowing Him to come in. Overcoming the spirit of the crowd is up to you. Choose to come up a little higher just as Zacchaeus did, and receive Jesus into your house today! ↝

A Conspiracy in the Church
(John 12:9-11)

PASTOR TERRY WHITE
Marsalis Avenue Baptist Church
Dallas, Texas

I believe the word "conspiracy" initially evokes a collage of different images in one's mind. When I think about a conspiracy, my mind envisions a group of people planning in secret to commit an illegal or subversive act. I think about those who act in a cunning and conniving manner to plot against, violate, intimidate, or assault another. When I think about a conspiracy, I visualize people slipping away under the cover of nocturnal darkness, hiding in shadowy places, and discussing subversive objectives. When I think about a conspiracy, I wonder about those things they would be ashamed of if someone else heard them.

Who would ever think about a conspiracy occurring in the church? After reading this passage, I wondered (that is, if my imagination works the same way as yours) if those who labored so diligently to canonize the Scriptures and translate them into the form we have today would have permitted such an event to slip into the pages of Holy Writ.

But after careful thought, it does appear to me that there actually was a conspiracy taking place in this passage. Throughout the history of mankind, we know of conspiracies that involved the deaths of eminent persons in our communities. But could it have been possible for such an occurrence to actually happen in the days of Jesus?

WHY DO YOU WANT TO MURDER LAZARUS?

After reading this passage, I realized that these chief priests were involved in a conspiracy. You probably would say to me by now, "If all that you say is true, what is the relevance of discussing this conspiracy today? What relevant, applicable information can we gain from this incident in the lives of some local citizens of Bethany? And even if you have uncovered a conspiracy, preacher, why bother to discuss it in this 21st century time period?"

There must be several good reasons ensconced within the context of this text—especially if they were serious enough to provoke the chief priests and religious leaders, who were examples of moral excellence in the community—to participate in a conspiracy plot to murder Lazarus.

Let's analyze the rationale involved on the part of these chief priests. They were the ones who stood up on the Sabbath day and declared, "Thou shalt not kill," yet this Spirit-inspired record reveals that these same examples of moral excellence were closeted in dark places in temple territory to discuss putting out a contract on one of the local parishioners. So, we can safely conclude that there is a conspiracy present in this passage of Scripture.

The text does mention that the chief priests were involved. The chief priests consulted together regarding how they might put Lazarus to death. A conspiracy simply defined is nothing more than a discussion about an attempt to violate and assault another person, and that's what we find on the agenda of these chief priests. I was concerned about what this Brother Lazarus did that caused the local priests to decide that he would be better off dead. There had to be a good reason for the local religious leaders—these chief priests of the church hierarchy who were the epitome of piety in the community and given the opportunity to mold and shape lives—to consult together to put Lazarus to death. I was concerned about whether or not Lazarus had violated some law that I had not heard of. I also wondered if perhaps the record had left out a gap of information about the life and character of Lazarus of Bethany regarding some skeletons in his closet. Perhaps there was some biographical information about Lazarus that was never exposed.

Actually, Lazarus was the brother of two young sisters who lived in the hamlet of Bethany. It was a suburb located outside of Jerusalem, geographically situated on the shoulders of the Mount of Olives. In Bethany, these three shared a bond of kinship: Mary, Martha, and Lazarus. When Lazarus became ill, Mary and Martha sent an urgent message to Jesus about the failing health of their brother. What did Lazarus do to provoke the anger of these chief priests?

If anyone had developed a level of tolerance, it should have been these chief priests. If anybody knew how to forgive, it should have been these chief priests.

It also stirs up a measure of curiosity on our part when we consider that these chief priests were willing to jeopardize the eternal destiny of their souls to discuss a murder plot concerning a local member.

You don't casually talk about murdering someone, because homicide is a very serious matter, both legally and spiritually. To think that these chief priests were discussing the murder plot of Lazarus! There must have been a good reason, if the priests were sitting down and plotting the killing of Lazarus.

But, you will discover that Lazarus had not violated any law nor offended anyone. Lazarus was not a revolutionary, he was not an insurrectionist, and he had no criminal record. So the question arises, "Why would these chief priests discuss a plot to kill a brother in the neighborhood?" What prompted chief priests, the holy men of God, to involve themselves in Murder, Inc.?

RESPONDING TO JESUS' POWER MAKES YOU A TARGET

This story gets interesting because Lazarus was not even popular. Lazarus' name probably would not have made it in the Book of John if he had not been a subscriber to the natural law. Lazarus became known because he died during Jesus' ministry years. If Lazarus had not died during that time period, it is very possible that he would have never been mentioned in John's Gospel account. As a matter of fact, on another occasion, when John wrote about Jesus' visit to these two sisters in Bethany, he did not mention Lazarus at all. There are some commentators and theologians who doubt the historicity of Lazarus because he was not mentioned until the 11th chapter of John. Thus, Lazarus had not offended anyone; all he did was "die." So what prompted this conspiracy to destroy Lazarus?

I envision this episode in the life of Lazarus as a kind of preview for those of us who allow our lives to respond to the power initiated by Christ. I believe this story is relevant today in Christendom regarding what will happen and what does happen to any person who allows himself or herself to become a usable instrument for the work of kingdom-building. It's evident to me that the church and all of its leaders are becoming candidates for conspiracy. Every congregation that allows itself to be used by the power of God makes itself vulnerable to become the victim of a conspiracy. I think I ought to warn those of you who have given up the fight and become complacent that there are those still hiding in secret places who are involved in discussing the murder of any person who endeavors to exemplify the marvelous might of the Master.

The Scriptures share with us that on the eve of the crucifixion, Lazarus was a living testimony of this One called the Christ. He was a local testimony as well, a focal point for those looking for the Prince of Peace. These chief priests didn't like that. They were frustrated about this Lazarus fellow. They felt that Lazarus would become a local tourist attraction if they allowed him to remain in Bethany as a testimony of the power of Christ.

Therefore, Lazarus had become somewhat of a hero in the neighborhood. Verse 9 says that many of the people knew Jesus was visiting with Mary and Martha. But notice that they came not for Jesus' sake, but that they might see Lazarus too. It appears that the priests were right on target with their suspicions: Lazarus had become a local hero. They wanted to get rid of Lazarus because the people wanted to look at him from time to time. They wanted to see this man Jesus had raised from the dead.

Thus, this conspiracy was prompted by the power of Christ, which always gets attention. Satan has built into the network of society a structured movement of conspirators waiting to plot and plan even the downfall of the church. Whenever the minds and hearts of men are being turned toward the direction of Christ, Satan launches a new offender. When people of God decide to become F.A.T. (faithful, available, and teachable) in the church, Satan dispatches an attack. Some people would like to discount Satan, but Satan is alive and well.

In fact, Satan is still operating with the same agenda; his itinerary has not changed since the ups and downs of Job. In the first chapter of that Old Testament book, Satan showed up in the midst of a conference with the sons of God and was questioned about his agenda for the day. He indicated that he was moving with ferocity, seeking whom he may devour, deceive, destroy, and disconnect. I just want to remind you that

Satan is still operating, and he very often uses the chiefs among us to conspire against the very power of Christ.

Satan understood that Lazarus was good evidence of the resurrection power of Christ. Satan knew that the people of Bethany were saying, "Maybe there is something to this Jesus fellow after all." I don't doubt that when Lazarus walked down the street, the children said to each other, "That's him. That's Mr. Lazarus." These chief priests didn't like it, so they plotted to kill Lazarus.

Then, I began to wonder what happened to cause these chief priests to think this way. Even if they killed Lazarus, had they suffered from a case of amnesia? After all, this was not Jesus' only miracle.

THERE'S ALWAYS ANOTHER MIRACLE TESTIMONY

Even if they killed Lazarus, what about that crowd of 5,000 Jesus fed out in the desert called Decapolis? Even if they killed Lazarus, what about those people who had watched Him multiply the contents of a little boy's lunch into a massive banquet? Even if they killed Lazarus, what about those people who watched the masterful techniques of Jesus exemplified in the desert with the hungry masses?

Even if they killed Lazarus, what about that fellow who had lain at the pool of Bethesda for 38 years until Jesus said, "Get up off your bed and carry your bed away"? Even if they killed Lazarus, what about that woman who had an issue of blood for 12 long years? She probably told people, "I didn't even have a chance to have an audience with Him, but I am well now. All I had to do was reach out and touch the hem of His garment."

Even if they killed Lazarus, what about that blind man who sat by the road at Jericho? Jesus had come by and made an ophthalmological salve out of the dirt and then anointed the man's eyes. He came forth from the pool crying and saying, "I have no technical explanation for what happened in my life, but I can give you a common explanation: whereas I once was blind, now I see."

Even if they killed Lazarus, what in the world did they plan to do with the woman whose boy had been lifted from the portals of death? One day, Jesus was passing through Nain, where He met a widow who was weeping and mourning about the death of her son. The undertaker and funeral procession were approaching, and the grave was opened, awaiting the arrival of the funeral entourage. Jesus halted the funeral procession and turned it into a family reunion. Even if they killed Lazarus, what did they intend to do with this woman and her son?

LIVING UNDER THE SHADOW OF REPLACEMENT

I often wonder how Satan drives the thinking of his instruments who allow themselves to be used by him. There are those who feel that the whole scheme of ministry is contingent upon one personality: THEM! Some people believe that nobody else can do what they can do. Sometimes in the arrogance of their own self-righteousness, they start to believe that the movement of ministry revolves around their own participation. Yet, God has His own persons waiting to be used by Him.

But, however we operate, it does not matter how eloquent we are, how melodious our singing, or how skilled we are in playing musical instruments: all of us operate in the shadow of replacement. I hear the Master saying, "I have the capacity to replace you. My program is not contingent upon one person. So what if you conspire to kill one of My servants? My project of salvation is not contingent upon the involvement of one personality." For so long, people have felt that if they could just kill the manifestation of the dream, then the dream would die. Many have felt that if they could just kill the examples of the power, the power would diminish. But no conspiracy can void the salvation of the Lord.

Yet, these chief priests still thought this latest physical evidence of the power of Christ should be destroyed. After four days, Jesus went to redeem Brother Lazarus from the clutches of death, and these chief priests didn't like that at all. Likewise, when you allow your life, your work, and your ministry to become a source of testimony for the power of Christ, there are going to be those who do not like it. Lazarus didn't do anything but respond to the power of Christ. When you respond to the power of Christ, people will get angry with you. Even within the local church, conspiring cliques and groups are operating subversively to destroy the reputation of the individual who responds to the power of Christ.

So, I'm not surprised about these chief priests who were behind this conspiracy, nor would I be surprised if these chief priests had some descendants in our local churches. But these chief priests were hiding in the temple, perhaps very close to the altar. Perhaps they were inches away from the mercy seat. And here they were, conspiring on holy ground to kill Lazarus. What a shame to even think of such a case! These chief priests were talking about killing Lazarus, and he had just been permitted to return to the land of the living. Again, Lazarus had allowed his life to respond to the power of Christ.

These sisters of Lazarus had called Jesus to come and heal him; but He didn't come immediately, so Martha was disgruntled. She said to Jesus, "If You had been here, my brother would not have died." She said, "If you had only come when we called for You, our brother would not have died." But I hear the Master respond, "Show Me where you laid him." Jesus went to the cemetery, and there He stood, looking into the eyes of His Father with a celestial gaze and speaking a divine dialogue. I hear Him saying, "Father, you have heard Me time and time again, and I need you to be God in Me. I'm standing at the graveside of My brother Lazarus." The Bible says that He stood there before death and the grave. Jesus said, "Lazarus! Oh Lazarus! Come forth from the grave." The Lord called him, and he walked away from the grasp of death.

Some theologians have suggested that Lazarus was in the anteroom of the "getting up" morning. While he was there, he enjoyed conversation with the old patriarchs. While he was there, he was resting in the bosom of Abraham. While in the midst of one of his Paradise conversations, Lazarus heard a voice ringing down the corridor of eternity. He heard a voice, and I would imagine, if all that was true, Lazarus must have said to those whom he was talking to, "HUSH! Somebody is calling my name." And Lazarus came forth from the grave. The Lord said, "Loose him and let him go."

We don't know whether they killed Lazarus or not, but even if they killed Lazarus:

- Peter was still waiting to preach on the day of Pentecost.
- Three thousand souls were waiting to join the church that day.
- Paul was still waiting to proclaim the gospel on Mars' Hill.

- John was still waiting to say, "I was in the Spirit on the Lord's day."
- There was still a Martin Luther waiting to lead the Reformation.
- There was still a St. Augustine waiting to come along and preach his sermons.
- There was still a Martin Luther King Jr. to come and say, "I have a dream."
- There was an African American, Barack Obama, waiting to become president of the United States of America.
- There was still a boy from Stamps, Arkansas, waiting to stand up at the age of six after hearing, "Come ye that love the Lord, and let your joy be made known" to accept Jesus Christ as his personal Savior and later to preach the gospel.

I came to Jesus as I was—weary, worn, and sad—but I found in Him a resting place, and He has made me glad. I don't know how you feel about it, but I'm glad that Jesus died for my sins. But, most of all, I'm glad that He arose bright and early on the morning of that third day and declared, "All power in heaven and in earth is in My hands." ᴄⅎ⌐

Restitution: Thus Saith Deity to Humanity

(Leviticus 6:17; Exodus 22:1-9)

DR. FREDERICK WILLIAMS SR.

Presiding Bishop
Gethsemane Worship Center
Albany, GA

On June 20, 1995, the Southern Baptist Convention voted to adopt a resolution renouncing its tolerance of racism and apologized for its past defense of slavery. On its opening day the convention altered the planned order of business in order to consider the statement of repudiation and repentance. As a form of restitution the Southern Baptist Convention, on its 150th anniversary, established a resolution deploring racism in all of its forms. This resolution confirmed, with respect to salvation through Christ, that "there is neither Jew or Greek, there is neither slave or free, there is neither male or female, for (we) are all one in Christ Jesus" (Gal. 3:28 NKJV). Furthermore, the convention resolved to repudiate the historic acts of evil such as slavery.

Inaction on this issue in the past has resulted in our reaping of a bitter harvest in the present. The racism in our society today is inextricably tied to the past. Within the content of that convention resolution is the foundation principle of restitution.

As defined in God's Word, restitution is the act of restoring to the rightful owner something that has been taken away, stolen, lost, or surrendered. The act of rendering an acceptable equivalent for injury demonstrates restitution. Also, simply a return or restoration to a former position or condition constitutes restitution.

Here, within this passage, we discover that stealing involves more than just taking an object away from someone. Finding something and not returning it or refusing to return something borrowed also constitutes theft.

RESTITUTION: MAKING WRONGS RIGHT

In Exodus 22, we find examples of the principle of restitution, which is simply the act of making wrongs right. God was taking potential situations and showing how His laws would work in the Israelites' everyday lives. His law listed here does not cover every possible situation; through practical examples, however, we are better able to decide what God wants.

What do you do when an apology is not enough? Sometimes it is not. The hurt has gone deeper, the betrayal has been devastating, and promises have been broken.

In verse 1, an example is given: If a man steals an ox or a sheep, kills it, or sells it, he shall restore five oxen for one ox and four sheep for one sheep. Practically, it offers the idea that if we have wronged someone, we should go beyond what is expected to make it right. We must remember that this is a sin against God and not just our neighbor.

If things have been acquired deceitfully, one must first confess his sin to God. He must then apologize to the owner and return the stolen items, with interest.

RESTITUTION: PAVING THE WAY TO HEALING

Many people have unfinished business in the kingdom of God. They are guilty of committing many wrongs that have never been made right. As a result, people are still angry and hurt. They are victims of a cycle of misbehavior leading to pain. The healing cannot take place because the guilty one has not paid restitution (God's way).

In Matthew 22:21 (NIV), Jesus talked to the religious leaders about paying what is due: "Give to Caesar what is Caesar's; and to God what is God's." When they heard that, they were amazed. They did not feel that Caesar should receive their restitution because he established practices that they did not agree with. Caesar was not a particular person;

this term was also used to describe the emperors or the Roman Empire itself (Augusta, Tiberius, Claudius, and Nero).

RESTITUTION: HOW MUCH DO I OWE GOD?

My final question is one that must really be considered: How much do I owe God? Just as He forgave me, I owe it to Him to pay the restitution of forgiveness to others who trespass against me. Christ saw my needs above my faults. My restitution to Him, therefore, must be to see the needs of my brothers and sisters.

David said in Psalms 116:12 (NKJV): "What shall I render unto the Lord for all His benefits toward me? I will take up the cup of salvation and call upon the name of the Lord. I will pay my vows to the Lord now in the presence of all His people."

How much do I owe the Lord? I owe Him enough to love and obey Him when He says to love my neighbor as myself. My debt to God is so great that I will be crucified, just as Jesus was for my redemption. As Paul said, "I am crucified with Christ: nevertheless I live; yet not I, but Christ liveth in me: and the life which I now live in the flesh I live by the faith of the Son of God, who loved me, and gave himself for me" (Gal. 2:20 KJV).

Acts 3:19 says that when we repent, God promises not only to wipe out our sins, but also to bring spiritual refreshing. We must go beyond the norm and hear God as He gives us a better way to repent and be restored.

Hosea 6:3 promises, "As surely as the sun rises, He shall appear like the winter rains that washes the earth and the spring rain that waters the earth." Do you need to be refreshed? The time is coming when God will restore everything. Go on and pay what you owe. Throw in the towel, for great will be your reward. ☙

A Dialogue with Death
(*Luke 24:6-7*)

———o∿o———

THE REV. JOHNNY RAY YOUNGBLOOD
Mt. Pisgah Baptist Church
Brooklyn, New York

"He is not here, but is risen. . ."
(Luke 24:6 KJV)

This is the news dropped by some celestial messengers to some sorrowing sisters who had made their way to the Savior's sepulcher on a given Sunday morning.

The angels said to the sisters, "He is not here, but is risen."
And the only explanation offered by these celestial creatures is in the form of the memory-jolting pronouncement found in Verses 6b and 7, where they said, "Remember how he spake unto you when he was yet in Galilee, saying, The Son of man must be delivered into the hands of sinful men and be crucified, and the third day rise again."

In other words, my brothers and sisters, I hear the angels saying to the ladies, "Didn't He tell y'all He wasn't going to be here?"

You see, my brothers and sisters, when the S-U-N rose that morning, the S-O-N had already risen.

These sisters and certain others were already suffering from the horrible hangover of Jesus' crucifixion. They had, under extreme anguish, recognized the historic Sabbath. And now, motivated by that love that defies even the power of death, they beat a path to the burial site of Jesus. There, as the victims of honest unbelief and pitifully short memories, they discovered the missing *corpus delicti*. They found the stone rolled away, but reasoned that some of the bereaved who arrived earlier had moved the stone. But then, after the discovery that the body was not there, John's record and Mark's memoirs implied that so sinister were the protectors of the status quo—the Roman government—that one of the women concluded that the corpse had been confiscated: "They have stolen my Lord's body."

Then, they were informed by an angelic presence, "He is not here, but is risen."

Can't y'all hear it? The angel is implying, "You're not at the wrong tomb, sisters. He was here; He just ain't here now. No one has taken Him. Though you're early, you're late! You woke up early, but He rose even earlier. Sisters, not only has the S-U-N risen as it is accustomed to do, but just like He said He would, the S-O-N has also risen."

WHAT HAPPENED AT THE TOMB?

Now, my brothers and sisters, I am a spiritual snoop. Whenever I read the Scriptures, I'm always looking for some spiritual scoop. I wanted to know what happened. I needed more information than that which came from some creatures from another realm telling these sisters, "He is not here, He is risen." Somebody, I felt, needed to give me more information on *my* Savior than just the statement, "He is not here, but is risen." *I wanted to know what happened.* I know that He'd already said He wasn't going to be a permanent resident of the silent city. I know He said that! And I know He had never been caught coming up short on His word. But I still feel as a member of the family that, especially by faith, there's got to be more of an explanation to the missing *corpus delicti* than just some creature from another realm coming along making the announcement, "He is not here, but is risen." And so, I am determined in the power of the Spirit that somebody must talk to me about my Savior's missing body.

Let's examine for a few minutes who was on the scene.

One writer reports that some soldiers were there, but they were so awe-stricken and amazed that they couldn't believe it; and their employers couldn't believe it either. Also, they had been ordered and paid to lie about the disappearance of the body. So we can't talk to the soldiers.

How about the angels themselves? No. Forget the angels. Don't try to talk to the angels because, you see, they are messengers of the Most High, and most of their appearances in the Scriptures are characterized as monologues. They do not entertain the queries of the creature; they merely deliver the message of the Creator.

How about Simon Peter? Naw. Remember, he followed Him from afar off.

Andrew? No! He was Simon Peter's youngest brother, always in Simon's shadow. So, most probably, he followed a little farther off.

What about Nicodemus? Nicodemus was probably somewhere moving under the shadows of the night.

And the women visitors? Remember that they got there after the fact.

Is there really anybody with whom we can talk about our Lord's missing body?

Let me explain to you one of the reasons why I'm determined to talk to somebody. There is talk of an alleged/speculated *resurrection*. And if such was the case, God was in on it. If God was in on it, He never leaves Himself without a witness. So, the logic of faith concludes that there's got to be a witness somewhere who can testify to what went down between sunset Friday and sunrise Sunday morning.

Q AND A WITH MR. DEATH

"God! Oh, God! God, with whom can we talk about our Lord's missing body? With whom can we talk about this *corpus delicti* that disappeared? With whom can we talk, God? Would you direct us to 'the witness' for a little while?"

And God says, "Why not talk to the star witness?" "The star witness?" we reply. And God says, "Yes, the star witness who is also the chief victim!"

"Lord, do you mean Death? Oh, yeah! Death, the now stingless victimizer of the living. Death had to be there!"

Wow! God Almighty is granting us an interview with the landlord of the household of the lifeless. Think about it: divinity allows dust to dialogue with Death. Let us take advantage of this opportunity.

"Mr. Death? Oh, Mr. Death, the Sovereign has granted us mortals permission to engage in an interview with you for faith's sake. We want to know about the conflict on Calvary.

"Now, Mr. Death, we know you're busy. The hearse wheels keep on rolling. We know you're busy. The church bells keep on tolling. We know you're busy. The obituary rolls are steadily swelling, and many cemeteries are plagued by overpopulation. Mr. Death, we know you're busy. Your movements are reported by the newspapers, relayed by the radio and beamed out on worldwide TV. Mr. Death, we know you're busy. But for faith's sake, **the Lawyer of the land** has given us permission to talk with you for a few minutes about what went down first-hand in the incident on Calvary."

Q: Oh, Mr. Death, pardon us for staring at you and for being a bit personal. But, Mr. Death, while looking at you, we noticed that you're not made up like other creatures. You lack certain anthropomorphic features. Mr. Death, there are some regions of your being that cannot be spoken of in anatomical terms. Mr. Death, why are you made up the way you're made up? You are a rather grotesque-looking creature. Why are you made up the way you are?

A: I'm made up the way I am in order that discrimination might not be one of my abilities. You see, *I'm blind.* I have no place for eyes or eye sockets in order that color consciousness might not control me. I'm blind in order that social status will be of no effect. You can be as white as the drifting snow. You can be as red as crimson or as yellow as the noonday sun. If you're from Mars, you can be as green as grass. If you're black, you can be as black as a thousand midnights down in a cypress swamp. But when it's your time to go, your color does not sway me. *I'm blind in order that social status might not control me.* I've pulled princes from thrones, and I've pulled paupers from gutters. I've got access to every house in the universe. I've got access to the White House, the courthouse, and the church house. I've even got access to your house. *I'm blind in order that discrimination might not be one of my abilities.*

But not only that, since you're asking, look close and you will see that there is no place for ears or any kind of hearing apparatus. *I'm deaf in order that last-minute negotiations might not sway me.* See, I can't hear, "Wait." I can't hear, "No. . .I'd like to see my children grow up." I can't hear, "Give me one more chance." I can't hear, "Let me get my house in order." I am not Opportunity. I never knock twice—maybe once. To be honest, I don't have to knock at all. No notices are necessary. I just show up.

And in case you don't recognize it, look closer since you want to know something about me, and the Almighty has given me permission to talk to y'all. If you had a stethoscope, that medical instrument, and you used it in that region that's normally known as the upper torso, you will discover that *I'm also without a heart.* I'm heartless. I don't have any regard for blood bonds. I'll snatch parents from children and children from parents. I've got no qualms about depriving nations of leaders. I'm heartless. I don't care who you are, how old you are, what you mean to somebody, or what you don't mean to anybody. When it's your time to go, it's your time to go."

Q: Thank you, Mr. Death, for those sobering realities. Would you talk with us a little bit about your background?
A: Well, Adam's rebellious act made room for me in creation. Haven't you read what it says in your Scriptures? Don't y'all remember? *By sin came death into the world.* And my presence and power has since been recognized. Why, since my debut, it has been once appointed unto all men to die. I've written that into the equation of human history. You see, what y'all need to accept is that I walk hand-in-hand with life. You don't die because you're old. You don't die because you're knifed by a maniac or you're struck by a drunken driver. You die because you are alive. If you don't want to die, then you don't want to live. You can't have a life without dying. That senior citizen at 80 is dying no faster than the junior citizen at 18. The senior might be 80, and the junior might be 18; but one merely starts earlier and the other one leaves a little later. The clock ticks away the same measured seconds for one as it does the other. And while I know you have the hope of being caught up to meet Him, you don't know whether or not that's going to be your arrangement. Most of you have a date with death and reservations in a cemetery somewhere.

Q: What are some of your affiliations?

A: Well, since Calvary, I've worked for God and the Devil, but a whole lot of y'all work for me. Lee Harvey Oswald worked for me, and Sirhan Sirhan worked for me. James Earl Ray worked for me. John Wilkes Booth worked for me. Adolph Hitler worked for me. Judas Iscariot worked for me. Some of the slavemasters worked for me. You need to know that each man and woman holds within their hands the power of death over another man. All of y'all somehow or another can kill each other. If you don't do it with a knife or a gun, there is a little pound of flesh that is a deadly weapon, locked up in the maximum security of 32 teeth. And even your Bible informs you that the power of life and death is in the tongue. Yeah, some of y'all work for me, and I've worked for God and the Devil since Calvary.

Q: Mr. Death, how do you see yourself?

A: Well, I've got a good record—a pretty influential reputation. It's not perfect, especially since Calvary, but I've got a good record. Upon my release from the solitary confinement of that tree in the center of the Garden of Eden, I got the run of the land. My debut was made when Cain, hostile toward his brother, sponsored me in that open field. And after that I got Abraham, Isaac, Ishmael, and Jacob; I got Moses and Aaron; I got Saul, David, and Solomon; I got Isaiah, Jeremiah, and Ezekiel. Hezekiah got a 15-year extension, but I got him in the end. And y'all rave about Methuselah who lived 969 years, but I still got him. In fact, you know what y'all need to know? Y'all need to know that I have an office in the halls of justice in heaven, and God—from time to time—calls a caucus on you mortals. And when He calls a caucus on y'all, I'm invited to the meeting with voting rights. I was there when we caucused on Belshazzar, and I got him. We caucused on Jezebel, and I got her. We caucused on Bull Connor, and I got him. We caucused on Saul of Tarsus, but mercy beat me out. We caucused on George Wallace, but it was a split decision; mercy almost beat me out. I got only his legs for a season, but in the end I got all of him. But y'all, I still got a good record. I got Ezekiel, I got Micah, I got Hosea, I got Isaiah, and I got Joel. I also got Matthew, Mark, Luke, and John. I finally got Paul, Timothy, John, and Mark. I got John F. Kennedy, Robert Kennedy, Abe Lincoln, along with Martin and Albertha King. I got a whole bunch of folks.

Q: But Mr. Death, haven't you missed a few?
A: Yeah, but you can't prove it. You're talking about Moses and Elijah, with their strange disappearances.

Q: Yeah, but there are some others, Mr. Death.
A: Who?

Q: Lazarus, Jairus' daughter, the son of the widow from Nain, and that Tishbite boy. Didn't you miss them?
A: I missed them one time. But, Youngblood, I got them on the second go-round. What y'all need to know is my record was all right until I got to Calvary.

Q: Mr. Death, we want to go there in a few minutes. But just one more question in terms of our preliminaries. Mr. Death, what is man's opinion of you?

A: I'm well respected; I'm even influential. Don't y'all know that it isn't until I threaten that some men get right with God? It isn't until I threaten that folks recognize how they've been wasting time and been mistreating one another. It isn't until I threaten that folks recognize the folly of riches and the limitations of family and friendship. When I threaten, a whole lot of y'all have gotten right with God. I'm well respected. And I'm influential.

Q: Well, last but not least, Mr. Death, we want to know what happened on Calvary. Mr. Death, you're kind of dropping what looks like your head. What happened on Calvary?

A: Well, since God has ordered this dialogue, I have to tell you the truth, the whole truth, and nothing but the truth, so help me. I can really sum it up in six words. I had no business being there.

Q: Say what, Mr. Death?

A: I had no business being there.

Q: What do you mean, Mr. Death?

A: Look, Justice moved that I should be responsible for dealing with those two men on those two outside crosses. Now, based on that, I should have been there, but I shouldn't have messed with that man on that middle cross. *I hate that I ever messed with Him.* In fact, since I've got to tell y'all about it, I was so mixed up that Friday I didn't know who I worked for—God or the Devil. But what you've got to understand is that those perverted politicians and those religious racketeers were always so willing to sponsor me that I took advantage of every opportunity to make my presence felt. *But y'all, I shouldn't have messed with that man on the middle cross.*

Q: What happened, Mr. Death?
A: He gave me a fit.

Q: What? We want some details, Mr. Death.
A: Well, since some of y'all claim you know your Bible, don't you remember that the wages of sin is death? *And He was without sin.* So, since He was without sin, *I had no business messing with Him* because the wages of sin was death and He was sinless. Not only that, don't y'all remember the promise from Moses' 90th psalm—that the days of our years are *three score years and ten (70), and if by reason of strength they be fourscore (80); yet is there strength, labor, and sorrow.* He was only 33. So based on the promise, *I had no business messing with Him.* Not only that, I couldn't even use His body as a vehicle on which to have disease to ride in order that His life might be snuffed out because He had more medicine in the hem of His garment than all the drugstores in town. What happened was this: I went up to Calvary that Friday, and I grabbed all three of them. Y'all, that man in the middle gave me a fit to the point that I had to *let everybody else go* just to deal with Him.

Let me tell you what He did to me, since I've got to testify. Let me tell y'all what He did to me. First of all, He wouldn't let me sneak up on Him. They tried to give Him something to numb His body—some anesthesia in order that I could sneak up and take Him away, but He wouldn't take it. In fact, when I went up, I rushed Him and blitzed Him. When I grabbed Him, He knocked me back and said, "No man takes my life; I lay it down." He wouldn't drink the potion that was given Him to numb His body. He wanted to present His body as a living sacrifice, holy and acceptable unto God which was His reasonable service. He wouldn't let me sneak up on Him.

And then I was there trying to kill Him, and He was up there *taking care of business*. I'm there trying to take His life and He's up there *giving*.

Q: What do you mean, Mr. Death?

A: Well, don't y'all remember that while He was hanging on the cross He stopped dying and gave a thief last-minute reservations on the evening train to Paradise? And then that wasn't enough. He stopped (Lord, have mercy!) and gave the whole world forgiveness. He said, "Father, forgive them for they know not what they do." And then, as though that wasn't enough, He looked down and gave his mama to John and John to his mama. I was there trying to *take* and He was up there *giving*.

And when I grabbed Him, I really grabbed Him. I grabbed Him, y'all, I'm telling you. When I grabbed Him, I had already let the two thieves on the outside crosses go. But when I grabbed Him, I had to send for back-up. And when I sent for back-up, I had to let everybody else that I ever had *go*. That's why John wrote that *the dead got up and went walking through the streets of Jerusalem*. I had to release Abraham. Abraham reached over and shook Isaac and Isaac, Ishmael; Ishmael, Jacob; Jacob, Esau; Esau, Moses; Moses, Aaron; Aaron, Saul; Saul, David; David, Solomon. . . .They all got up and started walking through the streets of Jerusalem. That's what it took for me to hold Him. I got Him. I had to let everybody else go, but I got Him. *But, I could only hold Him from sunset Friday to sunrise Sunday morning.*

Q: Then what happened?

A: Since I got to tell y'all the whole truth and nothing but the truth, let me tell you something that was so amazing. When I grabbed Him and it was time for Him to get up, the angels got in a hurry and wanted to come quickly. The speediest angel—somebody said his name was Raphael, I don't know—came and said to God, "Let me go down and get your Son." And God the Father said, "Oh, no! That's My son. I'm handling this!" And that's another reason why Paul wrote to the church at Rome—*that God has raised Him from the dead.* God raised Him! The angels may have rolled the stone away, but God raised Him. In my native Louisiana, they said that when they buried Him, they put a rock in a rock; and then they rolled a rock on top of a rock. Then, on Sunday morning when God the Father got ready to raise Him, He rolled a rock away from a rock; and there was a rock in a rock. And then a rock woke up in a rock and a rock looked up at a rock, and then a rock stepped out on a rock.

Q: We all know that story.

A: Yes, but you just don't know the intimate details that I'm giving you in this moment. When He stepped out of the grave, ah, your Savior got sassy. He stepped out of the grave, shook my dust off, looked back, and said, "Death, where's your sting? Grave, where's your victory?" And then He raised His hands and pronounced the benediction for all time when He declared, "All power.. ." Do y'all know what "all" means? It means, "All power is in My hands."

That's why when the women arrived that morning, they were told, "He ain't here. He's risen. He was here, but He's not here now." The reason the tomb is empty is that I just couldn't hold onto Him any longer. These are the unyielding facts—that you serve a risen Savior.

I know that many of you have crosses around your neck. You also have crosses in your house and everywhere. But the cross was the instrument of the Enemy. The real instrument of victory for the believer is not the cross but the empty tomb. To the cross they nailed His hands, riveted His feet, and placed a crown of thorns on His head. The cross!

There were three men crucified in that moment, but only one got up!

That's why the resurrection makes all the difference.

RISEN MEANS "ALIVE AND WELL"

Well, this concludes our interview with Death. We thank God for condoning this dialogue. I urge all of us to recognize that we serve a risen Savior. He did die, but He didn't stay dead. They did crucify Him, but He got up from the grave and He's risen. He's risen. as He said.

You know what risen means? Risen means "alive and well." Risen— victorious conqueror. Risen—offering new hope to all men. Risen— disarming the last enemy. Risen— King of kings. Risen—Lord of lords. Risen—no *corpus delicti*. Risen—an empty tomb. Risen —neatly folded grave clothes, which showed that He wasn't in a hurry when He got up. Risen— absentee tenant. Risen—a displaced stone.

As the hymn says,

> I serve a risen Savior, He's in the world today;
> I know that He is living, whatever men may say;
> I see His hand of mercy, I hear His voice of cheer,
> And just the time I need Him He's always near.
>
> He lives, He lives, Christ Jesus lives today!
> He walks with me and talks with me along life's narrow way.
> He lives, He lives, salvation to impart!
> You ask me how I know He lives? He lives within my heart.

But not only that: He walks with me and watches over me all night. I serve a risen Savior. Thank you, Lord, for Bethlehem. Thank you, Lord, for Calvary. But above all, thank You for the empty tomb. He ain't there—He's risen. Risen! Risen! Risen! Risen! He's risen! ✍

Runaway!
(Jonah 1:1-16)

———⌇———

DR. JOEL C. GREGORY

Professor of Preaching
George W. Truett Theological Seminary
Baylor University, Waco, Texas
Distinguished Fellow, Georgetown College
Georgetown, Kentucky

You may not remember her name, but you probably remember her photo with her wild eyes as large as saucers: Jennifer Carol Wilbanks. Four days before her planned wedding to John Mason, Jennifer disappeared on April 26, 2005. The town went crazy, her fiancé was a suspect, and CNN gave us the word every 30 minutes. On April 29, one day before the planned wedding, she called the police from Albuquerque, claiming to have been abducted and assaulted. They took her back home, and little by little, her story fell apart. Neither one had happened to her: she was just a runaway. Her story was as crazy as she looked. She was charged with deceiving the police. The runaway bride was not a successful runaway.

Emily the Cat from Appleton, Wisconsin, curled up inside a shipper container bound for France. One month later, Emily crawled out of the container after it was opened at a plastics plant in Nancy, France—hungrier and scared, but still alive. Continental Airlines gave her a first-class seat back to Wisconsin. Emily was not a successful runaway.

Recently, the covers of the tabloids told about the runaway parents of *Jon & Kate Plus Eight*, the Learning Channel reality show. Kate ran away from the sextuplets and the twins for 21 out of 31 days, and then Jon ran off too. No one knew where they were, and they were both accused of being runaways. The producers threatned to cancel the show, and the bloggers buried them. Jon and Kate were not successful runaways.

It doesn't seem like there are many successful runaways. Jesus' most beloved story, The Parable of the Prodigal Son, tells us about another unsuccessful runaway. He was the young man who went to his father and asked for his inheritance, then ran away. What looked like a first-class seat to the Bahamas wound up in a back alley in the Bronx.

Yet the most famous of all runaways got a book in the Bible, not a long book but certainly one of the most riveting. Jonah was the first inductee into the Runaway Hall of Fame. He wrote the book, *Running Away for Dummies*. Jonah is the Bernard Madoff of runaways because he almost got away with it, but he got caught. Jonah ran away to the sea, and like many sailors, he may have gotten a tattoo before getting on the boat. If you read Jonah's tattoo, what would it say? It might have said, "When you run away from God, it's not an easy thing to do."

This book has a lot of riffs, but its main message is available to anybody: you may try to run from God, but He will get you.

YOU MAY RUN

This book begins in an unusual way with the Hebrew word that meant "NOW," as if it was the continuation of an ongoing story: "And NOW the word of Yawheh came to Jonah." It is the story of those who came before Jonah, as well as the story of those who followed after him. As the reader, you get painted right into this story at its beginning.

Jonah takes the stage with no introduction. We don't know that much about him, except that 2 Kings tells us he was a true-blue Hebrew, a nationalistic prophet with prejudices down to the core of his being, who lived during the time of Jeroboam II, an expansionistic king. He only rooted for the home team—Israel. He was so bigoted that he believed God loved the Hebrews and nobody else.

We'd like to know more about Jonah. Here, he's just like a Richard Avedon portrait. It's only Jonah against a backdrop with nothing on it. We would like to know who his parents were, who his wife and his friends were, where he was, how God spoke to him, and when this all happened. Yet, this book only focuses on what we need to know, like Ernest Hemingway's prose—lean, spare, without an extra word.

The book begins with a word from the Sponsor. God says, "Go to Nineveh." Five hundred miles to the east, Nineveh was the biggest, baddest city around, but its distant geography wasn't the problem. Its natives were the most hated, rapacious, bloodthirsty, scorched-earth warriors that Israel had ever known. To go to Nineveh was unheard of. It would be like going to Tehran, Iran, and telling President Ahmadinejad, "Jesus loves you and if you'll repent, He'll give you eternal life," or going to Pyongyang, North Korea, and telling Kim Jong il before he launches another nuclear rocket, "Jesus loves you and wants to give you heaven."

It was an outrageous message that Jonah didn't want to take, and no one wanted him to take it. God was saying, "Jonah, go with the most offensive, obnoxious, objectionable, unthinkable, unacceptable message you can bring. Go to the banks of the Tigris. Go to the most anti-God city on the planet. Go to the city where its ruler Sennacherib trumped God's name and called himself, "I AM."

My friend Dr. H. Beecher Hicks Jr., senior pastor of the historic Metropolitan Baptist Church in Washington, D. C., said recently that you have not really preached until you have made a statement that offended somebody—one that challenges the assumptions of the prevailing culture. But that is what Jonah was asked to do, and he told God, "Thank you, but no thank you."

Without a word, Jonah ran as fast as he could go. Three times in verses two and three we are told he wants to get to Tarshish, a colony in southwestern Spain, exactly opposite in direction from Nineveh. That was as far away as you could go by boat; in essence, it was sailing off the map. God said to go 500 miles east, and Jonah said, "No, I'm going as far as I can west. I'm going to get as far away from God as I can—from anywhere He has an influence on anything going on." Twice in verses two and three we are told that he wants to get away from the presence of the Lord, Yahweh. If there was wet cement on the dock at Joppa, Jonah's footprints would have been pointing west, not east. The verbs themselves have all of the hustle and bustle of a runaway: "set out," "went down," "found," "paid," and "went." Jonah is a walking verb, a man on the go.

The interesting thing is that it looks as if he'll get away with it. Everything was coming together. Have you ever noticed when you're running away from God, that right at the beginning, everything seems to come together? Right at the time he got to Joppa, there was a ship there that would go as far away as he wanted to go, and he had the right amount of money to buy the right ticket. He got out his Master Card and paid twenty shekels to ride a donkey to Joppa—PRICELESS. On the dock, he paid five shekels for a falafel sandwich before he got on the boat. He bought a ticket to Tarshish—PRICELESS. He sent a text message to his brother back in Samaria and jumped on board.

HOW IS IT WORKING OUT?

Everything seemed to be working out for Jonah, or was it? We poor human beings are never more little or miserable than when we think that we're running away from God and everything's going well. In our pathetic smallness, we can actually psych ourselves into thinking that we are getting away from God. Yet, we are not as successful as we think we are when we run from God.

Last week I preached at the First Baptist Church of Hollywood, California. When they called to invite me, my first thought was that the name of this church was an oxymoron: First Baptist, Hollywood. It's just a 100-year-old big building that sits one block off Hollywood Boulevard with only a few people attending services each Sunday. They do their best as an outpost of heaven in the middle of. . .Hollywood. A few weeks before I preached, Reese Witherspoon, the internationally famous movie star born and raised in New Orleans, showed up alone and sat on the very back pew of this big church with a handful of people in it. Nobody knew how she got there or why she came. Thirty-three years old, involved in a messy divorce and a tough custody battle, this famous star now just sat there, alone. It makes you wonder what brought her there.

Are there any of you who have wanted to get away from God but found yourself in church? Truth be told, you may have thought this whole church thing is so lame. Sunday school—what a bore. Preachers, deacons, the Bible, and choirs: that's so not now. The truth is, you find yourself running away. God said, "Come to Me," but you have gone in the opposite direction. God will let you do that.

May I bring a word from our Sponsor? How's it working for you? Ask yourself honestly. And I don't mean to be unkind. I've been there, done that, got the T-shirt. Some people say, "I want to go out and raise hell," and they find out they're already in hell. How about you? Do you feel like hell? We are not as successful as we think we are when we run from God.

Where God is involved, however, there is always a BUT. The fourth verse says, "BUT, the Lord hurled a storm...." The ship was a bireme, with a ram on the fore and two rows of oars down either side with a single square sail rigged on the mast. It looked like the perfect way to get to Tarshish. When the tremendous storm was hurled against it, however, this boat is personified in Hebrew as if it were screaming, "I am going to break apart." The rudder called to the mast, "I am ripping apart." The mast cried to the prow, "I'm going to be blown away." What a mess!

Jonah should have known better. His own Bible, in Psalm 139:7-10, told him,

> Where can I go from Your Spirit? Or where can I flee from
> Your presence?
> If I ascend into heaven, You are there. If I make my bed in
> Sheol, You are there.
> If I take the wings of the morning and settle at the farthest
> limits of the sea,
> Even there Your hand shall lead me, and Your right hand
> shall hold me fast.

A runaway believer can make pagans look good. The terrified seamen on Jonah's boat were holding a prayer meeting. As Phoenecians and Syrians, they practiced polytheistic religion. In fact, they had a whole celestial country club of gods, so they cried out to Baal, Marduk, Isis, Osiris, Ra, and every other god they could think of. Their inward emotion was fear, and their outward cry was to their gods because these seasoned sailors knew that this was the mother and father of all storms.

And where is Jonah? He is down in the bottom of the boat in stage four, REM, double dose of Ambien, four-martini sleep, and they can't even wake him up with the storm. The Hebrew word used here for deep sleep, *radam*, is the same word used of Adam when the divine anesthetist put him under to make Eve out of his rib. Out. . .of. . .it. What an irony. The believer in the true God is asleep, and the believers in the false gods are having a prayer meeting on the deck. When you're running away from God, you're often asleep when you should be awake because a storm is coming.

GOD DOES WHAT IT TAKES

The language of Jonah is so carefully chosen. Just as God "hurled" the storm, this same Hebrew word, *tul*, is used to describe the sailors' hurling of cargo overboard to either lighten the ship so it would rise higher in the sea or sacrifice to the sea god. God hurled a storm, and all the sailors could hurl was boxes of cargo. When God throws something at you, you can never throw anything that is big enough back against Him. He has His standard-brand ways of getting your attention. Sometimes, He'll throw something at your money or your stuff. When He does, there's no book that you can throw back at Him that's big enough. When God throws something at your business to get your attention, you cannot throw a business plan back at Him that will beat Him. When God throws something at your health, you cannot throw any bottle of medicine back at Him that will beat Him. We poor, fragile, weak, mortal people think we can throw something at God that will beat Him, but He's a big God.

Nineteenth-century poet Francis Thompson, the son of a wealthy London doctor as well as a college and medical school graduate, wished to become a writer, but then he lost himself. He became addicted to the drug of choice of that day, opium, and lost everything. He became a street person and had to move in with a prostitute. People tried to help him, but he had already blown his mind on drugs. He nearly starved but all of that time sensed that God was chasing him down. He wrote a poem about running away from God entitled, "Hound of Heaven":

> I fled Him, down the nights and down the days;
> I fled Him, down the arches of the years;
> I fled Him, down the labyrinthine ways
> Of my own mind; and in the mist of tears
> I hid from Him, and under running laughter.
> > Up vistaed hopes I sped;
> > And shot, precipitated,
> Adown Titanic glooms of chasmed fears,
> From those strong Feet that followed, followed after.
> > But with unhurrying chase,
> > And unperturbèd pace,
> > Deliberate speed, majestic instancy,
> > They beat—and a voice beat
> > More instant than the Feet—
> > "All things betray thee, who betrayest Me."

When you betray God, everywhere you turn betrays you. When the TV and radio are off, when the iPod is not in your ear, when you are not at the mall or the movie, when you are alone in the absolute quiet of night, do you have the feeling that Someone is pursuing you? Does it seem like Somebody's there? You can almost hear the footfalls. That's God saying, "I want you back. I'm the Hound of Heaven." With unhurrying chase and unperturbed pace, God will stay on your heels, and you should thank Him that He's there.

Meanwhile, when you're running away from God, you get everybody into the same mess with you. You don't run away from God by yourself. You don't run away from God without influencing other people.

Runaways make a mess for everybody involved with them.

I'm a Texan, born and bred; when I be dead, I'll be Texan dead. But we Texans have a problem. Many of us think we're mavericks—that we're isolated individuals. No. John Donne said it well:

> No man is an Island, entire of itself; every man is a piece of the Continent, a part of the main; if a clod be washed away by the sea, Europe is the less, as well as if a promontory were, as well as if a manor of thy friends or of thine own were; any man's death diminishes me, because I am involved in Mankind; And therefore never send to know for whom the bell tolls; It tolls for thee.

> **John Donne**, *Meditation XVII*
> *English clergyman & poet (1572 - 1631)*

Thirty to fifty pagan, polytheistic mariners just wanted to sail over to Tarshish and get back; instead, they got caught up in Jonah's mess. They had to face his storm when they threw their stuff into the sea. Then, they had to hold a lottery in the middle of a tsunami to find out the culprit, the one who caused the storm. They had to turn into Larry King on the deck and interview Jonah with five questions to find out what to do. They wondered if they should try to row the boat back to the shore to put Jonah off when they would normally have ridden out the storm at sea. Then they had to worry about having blood guilt on them for throwing Jonah overboard because if he was innocent, then they would have to face God's judgment. No wonder they cried out to Jonah, "How could you do this?"

I recently preached with Dr. Cynthia Hale, the senior pastor of Ray of Hope Christian Church in Decatur, Georgia. She said, "If we sing 'This is my Father's world,' it means that I'm in a world with all the rest of His children; and if I have been graced, it's so I can go back and get somebody else out." Jonah had been graced, but he wanted to turn into anti-grace. So, he pulled everybody else into his own mess.

In the early days of cell phones in 1985, cellular technology was not what it is today. My first cell phone was as big as a suitcase. What was interesting was that I constantly got involved in other people's conversations. They bled into my conversations and confused me and the person I was talking with. That's something like what was happening on this ship. God was in a conversation with a runaway believer: "Come back!" But all of a sudden these pagan sailors got in the middle of Jonah's conversation with God, and there was nothing but confusion.

This is tight, but it's right: If you're running away from God, other people are involved—a disappointed spouse, shattered children, friends, roommates, neighbors, and church members. There are entire families whose children will be out of God's house and God's will for generations because of one runaway. What business partner have you taken down? You don't run away by yourself. When you run away, you always run away in solidarity with others.

If you were on wet cement on that same dock as Jonah, what kind of footprints would you leave? Would they be pointed toward God or away from God? None of us are immortal or eternal, but we need to at least leave footprints that point toward God, not away from Him. What an awful literary legacy Demas left when Paul had to write to Timothy about his one-time colleague, "Demas has forsaken me, having loved this present world." There he is for all time, one footprint in the very Bible. . .Demas.

When you are a Christian runaway, you have placed yourself in a ridiculous situation: you are both the problem and the solution. Jonah was the problem because he was disobedient; he was also the solution because down in his heart he knew that he was the only believer in the true God on the ship. The poor pagans around Jonah had no clue about what to do. They had to turn to the man who was the problem in order to get the solution.

One of the most bizarre counseling situations I was ever involved with happened many years ago in another place and time. A married professing Christian woman was having a secret adulterous affair. She asked me how she could try to win him to Jesus. She tried to be both the problem and the solution, but she could never be both.

There's no one more miserable than a Christian on the run. When you run away from God, there are people all around you that are in a mess because of you and do not have a clue what to do. You cannot really help them because you are the runaway. You are like a doctor who abuses his own health and gets sick and cannot practice anymore, a lawyer in trouble with the law who loses his license, or an accountant in trouble with the IRS over his own taxes. You need to be the solution; instead, you are the problem. When you decide that you'd rather be the solution than the problem, by God's grace you can be, and it will be a liberating day in your life.

THE WORLD FIGURES IT OUT

But if you are a runaway, the world will figure it out anyway. Jonah wins a lottery that he does not want to win. They bring him up from his stage 4 REM sleep onto the deck. Jonah is quiet; he hasn't said a word throughout all this mess. They're casting lots, or rolling the dice with different colored sides, which was standard operating procedure to discover God's will in the Old and New Testament. Proverbs 16:33 gives the background: "The lot is cast into the lap, but the decision is the Lord's alone." They figured that the God who runs the galaxies can certainly make a pair of dice fall where He wishes. (In the Asian culture the ancient practice of I Ching, in which the participants threw down a set of sticks, accomplished the same purpose.)

Here is Jonah, dragged to the deck by the captain to join the prayer meeting to the gods, and he finds himself a marked man. The thirty to fifty sailors cast lots in a process of elimination. Perhaps names were written on shards of pottery, and they were thrown on the deck until only Jonah's did not break. Somehow, he wins a lottery he does not want to win. The random casting of the dice points to him. If you are a runaway believer, the world will find it out.

Christian runaways are not good at it. One of the most miserable ways to live is to be neither in nor out of the Christian faith—neither fish nor fowl. They have enough of God in them to be uncomfortable in the world and enough of the world in them to be uncomfortable with God. They raise hell, but they feel like hell. That's what happened to Peter, who tried it while he was warming himself by the fire in the judgment hall when Jesus was on trial. Someone said, "I know you were with Jesus." Peter denied it, but his Galilean accent gave him away. Then he let out a whole string of four-letter words. He cursed, but I don't think Peter knew how to even say them right.

The pagan sailors put on a Larry King show on the deck. They asked him five painfully simple questions: "Why has this calamity come upon us? What is your job? Where do you come from? What's your country?

Of what people are you?" It's like asking him, "Who are you? Where are you from? Where are you going?" Jonah should have known how to act in light of his answers.

Dwight McKissic, pastor of the Cornerstone Baptist Church in Arlington, Texas, recently made a striking statement: "If you are still asking why you are here, what life is about, or where you are going, you are asking the questions of a child, not those of an adult." There comes a time when you know who you are in God, where you're from, and where you're going. Jonah should have known how to act in light of his answers.

A CREED WITHOUT A DEED

For the first time, Jonah speaks in verse 9. In the Hebrew version, there are 94 words before he speaks and 94 words after it. Right in the middle of this mess, Jonah finally does the best thing anybody who is a runaway can do—he tells the truth about who he is. He owns who he really is. He makes a public confession of faith that defines him: "I am a Hebrew (which is what the Jews called themselves to outsiders). I worship the Lord, the God of heaven who made the sea and the dry land." He defines himself as who he is. He worships the God of all gods, not some regional god like the ones the sailors were crying out to. That God made the very sea that is killing them.

When you define with conviction who you really are—"I belong to the Lord Jesus Christ"—it is a liberating moment in your life. You're no longer halfway in or halfway out, fish nor fowl.

For Jonah, his statement was good as far as it went. But here was his ultimate bind as being both the problem and the solution. He could recite the creed, but he could not do the deed. He professed a faith he did not live: "Oh, I believe in God, but I'm running away from Him as fast as I can." The amazing thing is that even the pagans look better than Jonah. They have a shipwide prayer meeting while he sleeps. They fear Jonah's God when he does not. Ultimately, in verse 16, they worship God, as well as sacrifice and make vows to Him while Jonah only goes overboard.

A couple of years ago, I was preaching at Marlborough Heights Baptist in Killeen, Texas, when I heard a pastor from San Diego give the most striking testimony of fighting the call to preach and then fleeing from God. It literally made him psychosomatically ill. Finally, his hair started to fall out in clumps for no known reason. He went to a Jewish psychiatrist, an unbeliever. In the session, the psychiatrist asked him, "Is God calling you to preach?" God will get you somehow if you are a runaway. He will do what it takes to make you own yourself, whether it is regarding salvation or vocation.

If you are a runaway believer, the world will figure it out, and you will be miserable once you are identified. The life-changing thing for you to do is to come clean. Stand up and say who you are in Christ. Disown your shadow self and own your real self. Jonah was living the life of a shadow self, not a real self.

In conclusion, God will get His way, so you might as well enjoy it. Here's the irony of the story of Jonah. The book opens with the statement, "*The word of the Lord came. . . .*", but Jonah, prejudiced to the depths of his heart, did not want to take that word to people outside his own little circle in Israel. Verse 16, however, says that a boatload of pagan sailors ended up fearing the Lord, sacrificing to the Lord and making vows to Him. Jonah, in his disobedience, did not fear God, sacrifice to Him, or make vows to Him. In fact, he had vowed to get away from God.

Yet, our God is such a big God that if you don't do what He wants you to do, He can take what He didn't want you to do and get done what He wants to get done. Only God can take your disobedience and get glory for Himself from it, so you shouldn't be miserable on the ride getting there. Why not own it and say, "I belong to Him."

You cannot beat God. Why run from Him? Why not instead run to Him? Why should you feel like hell and put everybody around you in hell when God will chase you anyway? But I know something better than Jonah because I know Someone better than Jonah.

- Jonah said, "I won't go. That was a calamity for others. Jesus said, "I will go." That was a rescue for others.

- Jonah said, "Throw me overboard" because he had to die for his own sins to calm the wrath of God. Jesus said, "Throw me on a cross" because He died for our sins to calm the wrath of God.

- In a storm Jonah brought calm by going overboard. In a storm Jesus brought calm by staying on board.

- Jonah came out alive of the whale after three days only to die in the future. Jesus came out of the tomb alive after three days never to die in the future. ☙

NOTES

NOTES

NOTES

NOTES

NOTES

NOTES